caring and sharing:

Becoming a Peer Facilitator

by
Robert D Myrick
and Tom Erney

Library of Congres Catalog Card No. 78-70543

ISBN 0-932796-01-X

Printing (Last Digit)

    30 29 28 27 26 25 24 23 22 21 20 19

Production editor—

Don L. Sorenson

Graphic design—

Earl Sorenson

Illustrations—

James S. Noreen

DEDICATION

IN LOVING MEMORY OF:

MARY ANN MYRICK (1912-1977)

Mother, teacher, generous giver and inspiration

REV. PAUL JACOB ERNEY (1906-1978)

Father, counselor, fisherman and friend

AND TO OUR CHILDREN:

MARK, SUSAN and KAREN

all former peer facilitators

MISHA AND CAMERON BEAU

peer facilitators of the future

PREFACE

In 1973 we began the *Peer Facilitator Program* at Bucholz High School in Gainesville, Florida. It was an exciting adventure, one filled with many rewarding moments and personal satisfactions. It was one of the most meaningful experiences in our lives.

We are sharing our experiences and ideas with you in the hope that you, too, will feel the challenges and the rewards that come from reaching out, caring for, and sharing with others.

Over the years, students involved in the peer facilitator program have reported that it has been one of their most significant school experiences. This book could not have been possible without their caring enough to share ideas about their work. As one student said: "I feel like I'm a part of something special—something that will have an impact on me for the rest of my life."

The program began as a result of the concerns related to the use and abuse of both licit and illicit drugs by young people in the community. A committee of parents, teachers, students and professors from the University of Florida met to discuss ideas and explore potential approaches to the solutions. Their efforts resulted in a program designed to train high school students in basic counseling skills, as well as provide them with information needed to correct many of the misconceptions and misinformation about the use of drugs.

The initial structure and emphasis of the program was altered later to include both developmental and remedial components. There is now a focus on working with others *before there is a problem*. Moreover, the scope of the program has been broadened to include work with elementary school students and adults in the community.

The program consisted of a class that met for fifty minutes each day. During the first nine weeks, students learned facilitative skills needed to promote positive growth and development. They learned by doing—trying out different techniques and activities that are eventually used with others. After completing the initial training, the students worked as facilitators with young children in elementary schools. They visited their assigned school at least three times each week for a period of seven to ten weeks, working with children individually and in groups.

The peer facilitator movement is the "wave of the future" in education. It is an exciting, energizing and relatively new movement—one in which you can become a part! You have the opportunity to make a contribution to the future of this movement and to help facilitate the lives of others by giving of yourself, by learning to care and to share even more than you have before.

RDM
TE

TABLE OF CONTENTS

List of Tables

Chapter I

I expect to pass through this world but once. Any good deed therefore that I can do or any kindness I can show to any fellow human being. . . let me do it NOW. Let me not defer nor neglect it for I shall not pass this way again.

peers
as
helpers

Welcome to what we feel has the potential of being one of the most significant events in your life. We are pleased that you have chosen to "get involved" by being a part of the growing movement of people helping other people. Your energies and efforts are needed in today's world. We believe you can make a positive difference in the lives of others.

THE NEED FOR HELPERS

Helping others in their attempts to make sense out of life is no easy task. Yet, reaching out and caring about what happens to another human being can be a satisfying and rewarding experience. So many people today are struggling to get along in this fast-paced and rapidly changing world that the need for helping services has increased in all areas, especially in the area of interpersonal relationships.

Take a minute to think about yourself and the people with whom you interact each day.

How many are pleased with their lives?

What about your own life?

How happy are you with what you have accomplished so far?

How optimistic are you about the future?

Many self-help books have been written over the years. They attempt to assist us in our search for personal happiness and contentment. These books, and related magazine articles, have been read by millions of people who are seeking more productive, satisfying and enjoyable lives. Interestingly enough, there are more and more indicators that many people are failing to live fulfilling lives.

Oscar Wilde, the famous playwright, perhaps said it best: *"To live is the rarest thing in the world. Most people EXIST—that is all."*

We are confronted with a growing body of knowledge that dramatically illustrates the problems of today's youth. Think about what these figures say about the stress, pain and tension that many young people are experiencing:

1. *More than 1,000,000 young people below the age of 18 run away from home each year.*
2. *Millions of young people are abusing the use of alcohol and other drugs. The Department of Health, Education and Welfare reports that one teenager in twenty has a drinking problem.*
3. *Suicide is the second-leading cause of death of people ages 15 to 24 .*
4. *In schools last year there were 8,000 rapes, 11,000 armed robberies, 256,000 burglaries and 190,000 major assaults.*
5. *Juvenile delinquency is increasing and one out of nine young people in the U. S. will be involved in the juvenile justice system by age 18.*
6. *Unwanted pregnancies among teenagers have increased and about 25% of all babies born today are to teenage-mothers.*
7. *Child abuse has become a major social problem.*

Many young people today feel frustrated, disappointed, angry and hurt. As a result, many of them are choosing to abuse the use of alcohol and other drugs to lessen the pain of living or give it some false meaning. Some, in attempts to demonstrate their personal power, commit violent and destructive acts. Out of loneliness and confusion, some strike out in ways that momentarily make them feel powerful and successful, only later to learn how self-defeating they were.

The world continually bombards us with a vast array of conflicting options from which to choose. And, in this ever-changing environment, there seems to be little stability. The relatively calm, dependable and predictable surroundings of the past have been replaced by a frantic, quick-changing and unpredictable present—a present that is full of anxiety and pressure.

Let's take a closer look. While the names of the students have been changed, the events presented in the following cases are true. Each one is seeking to live an enjoyable life; yet, the barriers often seem insurmountable. As you read their stories, how would you react if you were talking with them? How could you, or someone else, be of assistance?

THE CASE OF MARY

Mary is a junior at Riverdale High School. While going to school is not Mary's favorite way to spend her time, she does care about her classes and grades. In fact, she began the year with a "B" average in the college prep curriculum.

Mary's father is a science teacher at the local junior high school and her mother is studying for a real estate license. She has one brother who is ten years old, very athletic, and a "B+" average student in elementary school.

This year is a troubled one for Mary. At the suggestion of a friend, she began keeping a diary. The following entries tell us some of what she's experiencing:

October 14

"Boy, am I ever glad that today's over! I'm really getting tired of being yelled at and criticized—makes me feel like I can't ever do anything right. In math class today, just because I didn't do all of the homework, Mrs. Stewart used me as an example of someone who has a lot of ability, but is too lazy and probably will never amount to anything. I can't believe that she humiliated me in front of the whole class! Maybe I'll cut her class the rest of the week. . . .

Dave and I got into an argument at lunch. He keeps pressuring me. He keeps telling me that I really bring him down when I just sit there and don't get loaded. He may be right, but I don't enjoy smoking any more. . . . My grades are dropping. Missing too many classes. . . . Mom and Dad would kill me if they found out I'd smoked and skipped classes. . . . Speaking of Mom and Dad, I'm getting tired of their yelling and shouting at each other. Wow! What a yelling match they had tonight! They didn't think I could hear, but there was no way I could miss it. Mom threatened to leave him again and he just went bananas. Sure wish she'd quit nagging. She never lets him relax. She complains that we don't have enough money and then gripes when he teaches a night class because he's never home. . . .

I wonder if tomorrow will be any better. Sure hope so, cause I'm getting tired of feeling down. . . . Wish I could talk with someone about some of this, but I don't think my friends would understand. Their world is so different from mine. . . . Guess I'll just have to learn to live with it. . . . I wonder if I can?"

November 17

"Lots has happened since I last wrote. Don't have a lot of time so I'll just hit the highlights (or low points). Got my PSAT scores back yesterday and I really bombed. Can't believe I did so poorly, maybe I'm not college material after all. Is Mrs. Stewart right? Dad was so disappointed in me. He tried to hide it, but I could tell. Damn, why can't anything ever turn out right? I'll never get into college if I keep this up. Talked with Sandi today about her parent's divorce. . . she was crying and really scared. Both her parents want her to live with them and she doesn't want to hurt anyone's feelings. I told her that if I were her, I'd refuse to make the choice. Why do parents do the things they do?

I almost forgot. . . Doug called and asked me to go out with him next weekend. I really want to go, but I'm afraid that Dave will find out. Guess I could ask Dave how he'd feel if I went out with Doug? NOPE! That would never work. Maybe Dave will be gone next weekend and I can get away with it.

I'm getting anxious for Christmas to come. It'll be great to be away from school for fourteen whole days! No homework to do and no teachers to hassle me. That's all for now."

How do you think Mary will handle the pressure she is feeling?

What would you say to her if she were your friend and she let you read her diary?

What could make her life more enjoyable?

How could you help?

THE CASE OF NICK

Nick is a recent graduate who joined the Navy after finishing high school. He's now stationed in Italy and spends some of his free time writing home to friends. The following is a letter he sent to his school counselor, Mr. Collins:

Dear Mr. Collins:

I don't know if you've heard where I'm stationed, so I'm writing to fill you in. The Navy decided that I'd enjoy living in Italy, so here I am.

Navy life sure is different from going to school there at good old Gaineswood High. I have to get up at 6:30 almost every day, and I don't usually complete my duties until around 5:00 at night. So far I haven't had any opportunity to travel and see what it's really like here in Europe. Guess they want to make sure that I know how to work before they let me go out and "play." The only thing that really bothers me about being here is that I won't get to see all my friends and family for over a year. Oh well, I think I can survive.

Mr. Collins, I want you to know how very much I appreciate all of the help you gave me during my years at GHS. I still remember the first time I came to see you. My schedule was all messed up and you got it fixed for me. I knew then that I liked you because you really understood and were concerned about the mix-up in my classes.

I don't know if you remember how close I came to quitting school my junior year. I was ready to hang it up, but you really helped me to think about my future and what I was doing. I felt so out of place and my classes were so boring. If it hadn't been for you, I'm not sure what I'd be doing right now. Anyway, I want to say "thanks" for all the time you spent listening and helping me with my problems. I wonder how many other kids at GHS are wondering what to do with their future? Sure hope they all get a chance to talk with you.

I've got to get busy now, so I'll close. Say "hello" to Mr. Puckett for me. He's a really good guy and I'm beginning to believe some of his stories about the military. So true ! Also, I'd really appreciate it if you could get the school to send me a copy of the school paper each month.

> *Sincerely,*
>
> *Nick*

What about Nick's letter?

How many students are there at your school who feel close to their counselor? or a teacher?

What would have happened to Nick if he hadn't found some-one to listen to him and to support him when he was feeling down?

Some of the concerns expressed by Mary and Nick are common to young people today. Many are searching for someone who will listen to them. . . care for them. . . reach out to them. There will never be enough trained and certified professionals to help. Students need students. Students also need to learn how to facilitate each other.

WHAT IS A PEER FACILITATOR?

A peer facilitator is someone who cares about others and who talks with them about their thoughts and feelings. Rather than being an "advice-giver" or "problem-solver," a peer facilitator is a sensitive listener who uses communication skills to encourage self-exploration and decision-making.

Peer facilitators exist at all age levels and, while they work a great deal with their contemporaries or those who share a related stage of life, they can work with various age groups. No matter the age, the setting or the persons involved, peer facilitators have the same objective: to promote personal growth and development through a helping relationship.

WHAT THIS BOOK IS ABOUT

The following eight chapters are intended to help you become a peer facilitator. Chapter Two focuses on some of the reasons people behave the way they do. After this overview of human behavior, Chapters Three and Four will assist you in developing the basic facilitative skills of listening and responding.

The next chapter, Chapter Five, emphasizes feedback. It suggests a way in which you can let others know the kind of impact that their behavior is having on you. The process of decision-making is outlined in Chapter Six. Decision-making is important when helping people take some responsibility for what they want their lives to be.

In Chapter Seven, evaluation and accountability are discussed. How can you assess your work and the effect you are having on others? A lot of the information that you will need prior to working in a peer facilitator program is presented in Chapter Eight. Various peer facilitator roles are outlined, as well as practical suggestions from "veteran" facilitators. The final chapter consists of questions that explore some of the problems encountered by other peer facilitators and some thoughts about them.

At the end of each chapter you will find at least three different "activities." Each activity is designed to help you become more involved with the ideas presented in the chapter. Some you can do by yourself. Others require you to work with a partner or in a small group. The peer facilitator trainer can help you decide the best way to complete all or any of the activities. Later, you may want to draw upon these same activities as a part of your work with others.

Well, it's time to get busy and to start learning some skills and methods. Helping others is not an easy task. There will be times of frustration, doubt and disillusionment. But, reaching out and caring for another person can also be a most personally satisfying event in your life. Most important, while being a facilitator and helping others, you can also learn a lot about *yourself!*

PROBLEMS OF YOUTH

PURPOSE:

To give consideration to major problems being experienced by young people today.

MATERIALS:

Pencil/pen.

PROCEDURE:

(1) Looking at the eight problem areas listed below, decide which problem you feel is the *main* concern of young people today. Mark a "1" in the blank next to the problem.

(2) Continue to rank order the rest of the problems until you have ranked *all* eight.

(3) Pair up with another person and compare your rankings. Be sure to listen carefully to the explanations your partner gives for their rankings.

EIGHT PROBLEMS CONFRONTING YOUTH TODAY

_____ Achieving in School

_____ Getting Along with Parents

_____ Changing Sexual Attitudes in Society

_____ Feelings of Loneliness

_____ Use of Illegal Drugs

_____ Abuse of Alcohol

_____ Making a Career Choice

_____ Making Friends

NOTES TO MYSELF

PURPOSE:

To keep a personal journal of your peer facilitator experiences. This is one way of helping you to learn more about yourself. By reflecting on your experiences as you write, added insight will often result.

MATERIALS:

A spiral notebook or stenographer's pad; pencil/pen.

PROCEDURE:

(1) Put your name on the front cover. You may also want to put a design or picture on the front that symbolizes something important to you.

(2) Take notes on the activities you do in class. Especially write down any tips on how to use the ideas (e.g. activities) with others.

(3) Take notes on the presentations and concepts discussed.

(4) If you desire, you can also write down any thoughts, experiences or questions which are important to you.

WHAT'S HAPPENING WITH TODAY'S YOUTH?

PURPOSE:

To help you learn more about the problems facing today's youth and to become more sensitive about the needs of our society.

MATERIALS:

Any publication—newspapers, journals, magazines and so forth.

PROCEDURE:

(1) Find an article written in a newspaper or magazine (or any other media) that describes a problem that is confronting today's youth.

(2) Bring it, or a copy, to class.

(3) With another member of the class or a group, complete the statement:

"There is a need for young people today to. . . ."

(4) Put your material on a bulletin board or reference shelf for the rest of the class to see and use.

WHO AM I?

PURPOSE:

To promote exploration of what is important to you and how you came to feel and believe as you do.

MATERIALS:

Paper and pencil/pen.

PROCEDURE:

(1) Write an introductory paragraph to your *Who Am I* paper which presents most of your "vital statistics" (i.e. birthdate, birthplace, people with whom you currently live, their occupations and so forth). Include any other factual information which seems important.

(2) Focus the rest of your paper on the following issues:

   A. What you enjoy doing—hobbies, athletics and so forth.

   B. Significant events in your life.

   C. Major beliefs and values you hold and how you came to hold these beliefs/values.

   D. Questions/concerns you have about life.

   E. Your plans for the future.

You may put these issues in any order you choose.

(3) Be sure to proofread your paper to insure that it is an accurate representation of who you are.

Chapter II

*The greatest gift one can give to another is a deeper under-
standing of life and the ability to love and believe in self.*

human behavior and interpersonal relationships

"Why do I do the things I do?" Have you ever asked yourself
that question? It is a common question that we often ask, ex-
pecially when things are not going smoothly. No doubt, there
have been times when you have observed others doing something that aroused your curiosity and you wondered: "What
makes them do that?" or "How can they act that way?"

Human behavior is fascinating. We talk about it much of the
time. It's not only a popular topic of conversation, but it has also
been the subject of serious study. We still don't know enough
about it. Psychologists have been studying human beings and
their behavior for a long time. More often than not, their work
has led to more questions than answers.

There have been many books written about human behavior and there are many theories that attempt to explain our actions. This is not a book on *Everything You Wanted to Know About Human Behavior but Were Afraid to Ask*. Rather, we are going to select a few principles, concepts and ideas which will help you better understand how people learn, make decisions, change and develop their own unique personalities.

UNDERSTANDING HUMAN BEHAVIOR

Since this book is designed to help you work with others and to facilitate their growth and development, it is important to have some basis from which to work. Some concepts about human behavior can provide a foundation for building helping skills and techniques.

While there may be other concepts which might be helpful, the following eight principles provide some understanding of people and their behavior:

1. We all have basic needs.

2. Everything we do is directed to some goal.

3. Our self-concept influences all our behavior.

4. Our self-concept is learned and can change.

5. Our self-concept is influenced by the consequences of what we do.

6. We are always learning and changing.

7. Increased self-awareness leads to responsible decision-making.

8. We learn from each other.

Let's take a look at these principles in greater detail.

PRINCIPLE 1: WE ALL HAVE BASIC NEEDS

In order for us to have a sense of well-being and to experience some degree of success, there are several basic needs that must be met. When these needs are not satisfied, we do not function well. When these needs are satisfied, our productivity, personal development, relationships with others and general health are enhanced. The most obvious needs, of course, are those of food, water, elimination, sleep and shelter. These human needs are necessary in daily living and we often take them for granted. To these we might add the following which also have been identified as essential:

The need to be loved and accepted. Each of us wants to be accepted as we are. While we are similar to others in many ways, still we feel unique and we want this uniqueness appreciated by others. It is both frustrating and disappointing when we are accepted only if we please others. There is a warmth and strength that is beneficial to us when we experience an unconditional love. It is an experience that helps us say: "Hey, I'm okay and it feels great to be valued as a person."

The need for security. We learn and function best in situations where we feel safe and relatively free from threat. It's not fun,for example, to be in a class where we are afraid that what we say might be ridiculed, or where we feel secure only if our work is mistake-proof.

For fear of making a mistake, some people develop a shell around themselves in which very few are allowed to enter. Such a shell provides protection that gives them a sense of comfort, even if it is limiting and prevents them from reaching out and enjoying new experiences. On the other hand, when they no longer need the shell and feel secure from threatening forces, there is a special joy in living.

The need to belong. There is in each of us a need to belong to some kind of group. To be a part of a group gives us a sense of identity. It helps us feel accepted and often provides the kind of support that is needed to help reduce anxiety.

For example, there are some students who, upon arriving at school, immediately go to a favorite meeting place where they can converse with their familiar friends. They find security and a sense of identity by talking with the group. "Hey, what's happening?" is answered in a way that communicates understanding, a shared interest and acceptance. Moreover, there are some formally organized groups, such as athletic teams, language clubs, music groups, pep squads and so forth that also provide a source of identity and a sense of belongingness.

The need to be independent, to take responsibility and to make choices. One of our needs is to feel in control of our lives. This emotional experience of feeling in charge — of being able to be ourselves and not be a puppet on a string — is important. When this need is thwarted, we become devious, manipulative, self-sacrificing and defensive.

PRINCIPLE 2: EVERYTHING WE DO IS DIRECTED TO SOME GOAL

We want to maintain and enhance our personal survival. Survival characterizes the essence of all living things. For instance, a plant will turn its leaves toward the sun and its root system will grow toward water. This is much more evident when there is only a limited amount of water and sun available. Survival plays the central role in all learning and behavior.

We spend most of our lives trying to *maximize our pleasure and minimize our pain.* If this seems too simple, apply it to your own life. You tend to do those things most often that bring you some kind of pleasure or reward. You try to avoid punishment, whether it is physical or psychological. You will protect your physical self and you frequently take precautions to avoid getting hurt. The same principle is also true of psychological pain.

It is important to remember that we not only change ourselves to help us survive physically, but we will change our behavior and make decisions that increase opportunities for the "psychological-self" to survive. We each hold certain attitudes, ideas and perceptions about ourselves. These thoughts are organized and generally consistent. They persist over a long period of time and the term *self-concept* is applied to them.

PRINCIPLE 3: OUR SELF-CONCEPT INFLUENCES ALL OUR BEHAVIOR

Each of us have some kind of self-picture. This picture might best be descrbed as *I* or *me*. It is this self-image or self-concept that determines our behavior. No other person will ever come to know us the way we know ourselves. It is through the self-concept that we perceive the world. We feel. . . we think. . . and we act, based upon our perceptions.

Your self-concept can be composed of many forms: *I am* —your general nature; *I can*—your abilities; *I should or should not*—your beliefs and attitudes; *I want to be*—your aspirations and desires. You will behave in certain ways, depending upon how you see yourself. When you act in a way that is generally not your usual custom, or perhaps contrary to the way you would like to be, then the experience is a unpleasant one and you may begin to feel defensive, inadequate, insecure and even worthless.

PRINCIPLE 4: OUR SELF-CONCEPT IS LEARNED AND CAN CHANGE

Self-concepts are learned and can change, although change is usually slow and most often tedious and painful. Once the self-concept becomes consistent, it is most difficult to change because change brings threat, anxiety and fear of self-destruction. Yet, people can and do change. Peer facilitators help people change. In the process, they experience some meaningful changes in their *own* lives.

Some parts of the self-concept can be attributed to heredity (e.g. physical size, color of skin, hair texture and general physical features). Yet, we are greatly influenced by culture or the environment in which we live. Two children growing up in two different parts of the world—or even in the same family—might behave differently because their unique environments and experiences have influenced their belief systems. Each has a self-picture and behaves accordingly.

PRINCIPLE 5: OUR SELF-CONCEPT IS INFLUENCED BY THE CONSEQUENCES OF WHAT WE DO

Rewards and punishments play an important part in determining how consistent we behave and how we learn. We do those things that enhance our self-image. For example, if talking tough and getting into fights is part of how a boy sees himself— *a la* Charles Bronson — then that will be part of his behavior. Or, if being a scholar and investigating certain scientific hypotheses—*a la* Dr. Salk—then he will spend a lot of time engaging in research activities.

Much of what we do is shaped by our past as well as our immediate experiences, but *nothing influences the development of our self more than the consequences of our behavior.* If the consequences are satisfying and rewarding, then it is likely that those behaviors will occur again and even perhaps form a pattern or become a habit. On the other hand, if the behavior is ineffective and plays no part in meeting our basic needs or enhancing our survival, then it is likely to be disregarded and not become a part of our personality.

Perception determines our reality and behavior. One of the interesting findings in the study of human behavior is that "reality" is influenced by our self-concept. What is reality?

Suppose we were to show you a five-minute film and then ask you and others in your group to describe what took place. In a short time you would soon realize that your *perception*, while similar in many respects, might be slightly different from others in your group. Such variance in perception, for example, has made it difficult for witnesses in a criminal case to describe accurately what took place. *How we see things determines how we behave.* The question is how do we see things?

PRINCIPLE 6: WE ARE ALWAYS LEARNING AND CHANGING

Learning is not limited to the classroom. Learning is going on all the time in your life. When you are not reading this book, for example, you are still learning by watching, listening, talking with others—as well as interacting with your surroundings.

Learning is more than gathering and memorizing facts. It is more than learning information in a formal educational setting. It is the very act of living and surviving.

Even though we can see some very consistent patterns about our personality—and even though certain personality patterns are formed before ten years of age—nevertheless, we are always in a state of change. We are always moving to something else.

We can and do change, but change takes time. Even though we want to change immediately, still change can be slow.

PRINCIPLE 7: INCREASED SELF-AWARENESS LEADS TO RESPONSIBLE DECISION-MAKING

Through increased self-awareness, we can learn to resolve our problems at a more conscious level and to take more responsibility for solving them. If we have a sense of self-awareness, we have more understanding of the factors that influence us when we make a decision.

If you lack this sense of self-awareness, you may catch yourself alibiing, failing to take a stand or being unwilling to accept the consequences of your behavior.

The ultimate responsibility for making choices and living with them rests with us, as individuals. We cannot live a life for another person.

PRINCIPLE 8: WE LEARN FROM EACH OTHER

Most of our learning comes through interacting with others, whether it be through direct personal contact or through reading what others are thinking. People provide us with rewards or punishments. They help us form relationships that are important in our daily lives. They serve as *models* that we incorporate or reject. Without other people, learning is limited and would be bland, narrow and unimaginative.

If we are going to help people become more responsible for themselves and to help them feel more adequate, worthwhile and positive, we are going to have to make some special efforts in understanding them. This means that we must accept their attitudes as part of them, not that we necessarily agree with those attitudes or behaviors. It also means that if we are going to facilitate people to change, we cannot do it by pushing our world onto them and forcing them to agree with our perceptions and decisions.

This approach in helping—or *facilitating*—puts a premium on understanding and acceptance. It emphasizes that change comes about best when others gain insight through their *own* experiences, rather than through our experiences. It means helping others explore their world, who they believe they are, what they want out of life and what they are willing to do to get it. It is this self-exploration that is critical to the helping process. It is through *self-discovery* that a peer facilitator can be most helpful.

INTERPERSONAL RELATIONSHIPS

We are surrounded by people and we experience many different kinds of relationships. Some are casual and fleeting; others are deeply personal and involve more commitment on our part.

INFORMAL RELATIONSHIPS

For instance, there are some people in your life that you know only by appearance. You have never talked with them, but you have seen them on occasion. It might be a neighbor down the street, another student in school or a teacher who offers a class that you have not yet taken. While these people may play some role in your life, their impact on you is minimal. They are very much like figures in the background of a painting. They add to the scene, yet their role is almost nonsignificant. There is no communication and there is no attempt to help each other experience life.

PERSONAL RELATIONSHIPS

We will probably have a large network of acquaintants and friendships in our lifetime. For instance, each of us might have a pool of acquaintanceships that range from 500 to 2,500 people. Actually, however, most of us have fewer than twenty friends that we rely upon for close communication. The average American couple today has close friendships with about seven people. Even though you may have some close friends that you rely upon to discuss various matters, it has been suggested by sociologists and psychologists that not all of them will be effective helpers.

STRUCTURED RELATIONSHIPS

When you go to a store to buy a pair of shoes, the relationship with the salesperson is more involved, but still a casual one. You may or may not strike up a conversation. If you do, more often than not, your thoughts are related to the task of buying a pair of shoes and the conversation is limited to that topic. Although buying a pair of shoes is a personal matter and the salesperson is interested in helping you, the relationship is usually safely limited. It is not necessary to learn more about the other person's personality.

When you go to a doctor or dentist, you usually have a well-defined purpose. You are asking for certain professional services. After an examination, a few questions and a diagnosis, the doctor then prescribes or performs some kind of treatment. Again, the focus is usually upon a particular concern and you are relying entirely upon the professional judgment and expertise of the doctor.

We trust these people to help us because they have either the credentials or the job position to offer us some service. There are usually certain accepted forms of communication and behavior in these situations. Both parties understand the limitations, the task and the desire to speed things along.

There is an increasing number of articles and books being written which describe how people in our society feel alienated or apart from one another. Relationships of all kinds are encountering additional stress and strain. Relationships are becoming shorter in duration. It has been suggested that people are not sufficiently involved with others to satisfy their basic needs. More and more, people are leading fragmented lives and having trouble communicating with others.

HELPING RELATIONSHIPS

Unfortunately, in our society there is a tendency for helping relationships to be too impersonal and task-oriented. Studies of effective and ineffective teachers, for example, have indicated that those teachers who have a more personal relationship with their students tend to have a more positive impact. On the other hand, those teachers who have taken less of a personal interest in their students, even though they may be well-prepared academically and understand their subject, tend to be less effective.

All helping relationships can be improved by understanding the ingredients that make for effectiveness. Studies of teachers, doctors, counselors, ministers, nurses, social workers and many others involved in the helping professions have led us to understand the conditions that are necessary and essential for effective helping.

One important discovery about counseling and therapy was that the most significant part of therapeutic effectiveness could be accounted for independently of a counselor's or therapist's theory and technique. It was learned that when certain helping characteristics were present, clients tended to get better. When these same characteristics were absent, clients tended to get worse or deteriorate. This shocking discovery has stimulated more research in the area of interpersonal relationships and the conditions that are necessary for personal growth.

While much of the information that is now being collected is still puzzling, one important finding is that the ability to create the helping conditions does not exclusively belong to professional practitioners, such as counselors, therapists and doctors. Rather, nonprofessionals—those who are not professionally trained, but who have an ability to form helping relationships— can and do facilitate personal growth in others.

THE HELPING CHARACTERISTICS

Attitudes and behaviors are changed very little by advice, persuasion or threat. We experience the most change when we are in the presence of a helping person who is positive, understanding, tolerant, easy to talk with and who cares about us.

The relationship between a "helper" and a "helpee" can be a positive catalyst in its own right. No matter how knowledgeable we may be of human behavior, how many degrees we may have, our sex, our age or our experience, *the real heart of the helping process is the quality of the relationship.*

Several people have attempted to describe the characteristics of a helping relationship. Different words and phrases have been used in an attempt to capture the qualities of a facilitative person. For our purpose, we have selected five helping characteristics that will assist you in your work:

(1) Listening attentively

(2) Understanding the other person's point of view

(3) Accepting the person

(4) Caring enough to be committed and involved

(5) Being genuine

Let's look at these five characteristics in more detail.

LISTENING ATTENTIVELY

Listening is perhaps the most important characteristic in facilitating others. A good listener communicates both interest and respect. Listening seems like a simple thing to do, but often it is difficult to put into practice. For most people, listening is simply waiting their turn to talk. They see it as a common courtesy. But, this is not what we mean.

If you are a good listener, you will avoid jumping in to direct the conversation or breaking in to make remarks that take the focus away from the person who is talking. You will avoid being preoccupied with your own thoughts. You will not let your mind wander or anticipate what the person is going to say and then jump in to complete the idea.

However, good listening is not being *passive*. It is not waiting or sitting back until the person has finished talking. Rather, good listening is an *active process* where we are trying to understand what the person is saying. As skilled listeners, we do not let our own needs, values and beliefs interfere. We restrict some of our remarks in order to give others an opportunity to talk. Then, we let them tell the story in their own way.

Following the lead of the talker requires both patience and practice. You will not only want to listen to the words that are being said, but you will focus on everything that the person is communicating, including the physical behavior that goes with the words. This means using not only your ears, but your eyes— observing body language. You will be asking yourself: "What is the message here? What is this person really saying? What is going on in this person right now?"

Listening is essential no matter the task. It may be gaining simple information, having a casual talk in a group or encouraging a person to talk in depth about personal experiences.

UNDERSTANDING

Listening is the basis for understanding. While listening is absolutely essential in facilitating others, it is not sufficient in itself. Even the most interested and attentive person may still have difficulty helping another unless listening results in understanding.

Understanding is not classifying, labeling, judging or evaluting. Rather, understanding involves a "feeling with" the person. It is trying to see things from the other's point of view.

Some have suggested that it is "putting yourself in the other person's shoes." Understanding is probably more than that. It is more than assuming another person's role. *Understanding is also recognizing and describing the thoughts and feelings of others.*

The word "empathy" is often used as a substitute for the word "understanding." Empathy implies that you not only understand the ideas expressed, but you also identify the feelings that are present.

If you can "tune in" to others, you will experience a closeness that enables you to know them better. You will feel like you are really with them. There will be some "good vibes" generated. You will not only be sensitive to the words that a person uses, but to the feelings that accompany those words. It provides a meaningful experience for the person who is talking. It is also a unique and rewarding experience for the listener. Unfortunately, empathy or understanding is not a characteristic of the general population. Yet, it is an interpersonal skill that can be learned.

ACCEPTING

It is difficult, if not impossible, to accept and respect ourselves if we are not accepted and respected by others. Therefore, one of the important principles of facilitating others is acceptance. Acceptance means recognizing that the person is a unique individual and worthy of respect.

If we are going to enhance the self-concept of others, then we must create situations in which they feel relatively free from threat. Threat narrows and restricts behavior. It makes the solution of problems much more difficult. If, as a facilitator, you are accepting and non-judgmental, then a non-threatening environment will be created. Ideas and feelings can then be explored in more detail. The more we feel that we are understood and accepted by a facilitator, the more likely we will self-disclose and take risks in the exploration process.

While listening and understanding are important characteristics, by themselves they are not enough. They must be combined with a genuine acceptance or respect. This is not always easy to do. It is particularly difficult when we see others as being different from ourselves. There is a natural tendency for us to either ignore or reject those who are unusual or different. If this difference is threatening to our own self-concept, we become critical, perhaps even belittling or condemning. Our own need for self-esteem and security may interfere with our accepting and respecting others. The more secure we are, the more we are able to be accepting. Acceptance leads to understanding, and all of us want to be understood.

It is important to emphasize that accepting others does not mean that we condone or agree with their thoughts and behaviors. The basic idea of accepting people is recognizing that they are unique and are doing the best they can to satisfy their needs and get along in the world. Moreover, accepting does not mean that we are encouraging them to continue doing what they are doing. Rather, it implies that we *accept their feelings.* In addition, we recognize that they are the ones who must assume responsibility for their actions and for any changes.

CARING AND COMMITMENT

We may be a good listener, be accepting of others and, as a consequence, be able to have more understanding of what others are experiencing. The helping process, however, can only take place when a helper and helpee are committed to working together. Thus, one of the most essential characteristics of a facilitator is caring enough to be committed.

Commitment means getting involved—personally involved—enough to care about what is happening. Being personally involved does not mean that we will be self-sacrificing to the extent that the problems of others dominate our lives. Instead, it suggests that we care enough to give some of our time and energy to them. There will be some limits placed upon the time and energy that we give, but without caring and commitment on our part, the helping process becomes bland and lacks energy. Without caring and commitment, a facilitator experiences early fatigue. Those being helped begin to feel unaccepted, unimportant or they may think that their problem is too serious to resolve.

It has often been said that people don't care enough about others. We sometimes become so involved in our own personal worlds that we pass by others who are in need of help. Time after time, newspapers report stories of individuals who have been victimized by others, while people around them have done nothing to assist them. It is frightening testimony of what our society can become.

It is very reassuring to have people care about us. It is supportive to know that others will give us their time and are interested in what we believe is important.

BEING GENUINE

Facilitators must avoid playing a role. They must avoid thinking: "It's time to play facilitator again." If the helping process is not a genuine one, it confuses the persons who are being helped and it eventually makes them suspicious. Such suspicion, of course, creates defensiveness. Being phony in a helping relationship may be harmful. Feeling one thing and communicating the opposite is not facilitative.

Genuineness, although limiting by itself, can be facilitative. It sometimes makes unknowing helpers out of persons simply because others can depend upon them for an honest response. Some persons, even though they have worked hard, studied and practiced under instruction, will still not be as facilitative as others because they "play" at being a facilitator.

When you assume a role that is not characteristic of yourself, your ability to help others decreases and you may not be helpful at all. This brings us to an interesting point that you will want to keep in mind as you go through this book. There will be times when you feel awkward and uncomfortable and you will wonder whether or not you are being phony. Maybe you need more time and practice. With practice you can learn to integrate the helping skills into your own personality and you will feel more genuine.

Many of the skills that you are going to learn are not a part of our daily lives. It takes practice before something can become a habit. To illustrate the point, please get a pencil or pen. Write your full name five times as fast as you can. Do that now.

Okay, now put the pencil or pen in your opposite hand and again write your name five times as fast as you can. Do that now.

What was your reaction? Perhaps after you switched hands and read the instructions, you might have thought: "Oh, no. I can't do this!" What were your other thoughts and feelings?

It may have been a little uncomfortable for you when you took the pencil in the opposite hand. It may have seemed strange and unnatural, especially at first. Interesting enough, the task was the same for both hands. But, when you put it in your opposite hand, you had to approach the task with more thought. You had to concentrate on how to make the pencil move in the right manner in order to form letters. Even the attention you gave it may have caused stiffness—a forcing of the pencil. You probably paid more attention to the smaller details on the second try.

As you begin writing your name for the fourth time, however, you may have been getting a feel for it and it was not quite so strange. It would still take practice—a lot of practice—before you could write your name easily, automatically and with precision. But, you could probably become ambidextrous and learn to write your name equally well with both hands. Likewise, by practicing the facilitative skills outlined in this book, you will feel comfortable and congruent.

SKILLS IN INTERPERSONAL COMMUNICATION

The facilitative process can be learned. Although some people appear to be "naturally" more facilitative than others, that is not the case. They were not born that way. They probably learned interpersonal skills through modeling and other experiences while growing up. But, even these people can improve their ability to help others by knowing more about *communication skills.* All interpersonal relationships can be improved through better communication.

For example, do you know someone who seems to be a natural athlete? Some athletes, because of heredity, past events and the encouragement that they have received, are able to perform in sports better than others. Even these people, however, can be assisted to become better athletes when they receive the right kind of coaching. The coach will probably focus on technique and style, trying to capitalize on the athlete's strengths. Good coaches don't over-coach. Yet, they can add a few ideas, when practiced and incorporated, that will make a person a better performer. Some even become champions.

This book focuses on several skills that will help you in your interpersonal relationships. They are the kind of skills, along with the helping characteristics that have been discussed, that will be useful to you in all parts of your life.

There will be times when you will want to be a facilitator of others and you will concentrate on bringing to the situation the helping characteristics previously described. You will also want to use the most effective communication skills. Listening, selectively responding, giving feedback — both praising and confronting—and making decisions are part of the facilitative process. Each of these concepts are dealt with in more detail in the following chapters.

Activity 2.1
UNFINISHED SENTENCES

PURPOSE:

To help you explore some of your attitudes and beliefs.

MATERIALS:

Pencil/pen.

PROCEDURE:

(1) Complete the following unfinished sentences:

    A. Helping is . . . .

    B. Caring is . . . .

    C. The most important quality of any good friend is. . . .

    D. If I had a problem, I would feel most comfortable talking with . . . (name) because. . . .

    E. Young people who become involved in illegal activities do so because. . . .

(2) In groups of four, share your responses to the unfinished sentences and explore your ideas and feelings.

Activity 2.2
FIFTEEN THINGS I LOVE TO DO

PURPOSE:

To look at what you prize and cherish about life. By examining a list of things you love to do, you can enhance your self-knowledge and stimulate your desire to act.

MATERIALS: An 8½ x 11-inch sheet of paper; pencil/pen.

PROCEDURE:

(1) Draw a line down the middle of your paper.

(2) On the left side of the paper, list *Fifteen Things in Life That I Love to Do.*

(3) After completing your list, divide the right side of your sheet into five narrow columns.

(4) Now, code your list in the following manner:

A. Put a "$" sign beside any item which *costs* more than $5.00 each time you do it.

B. Put an "R" beside any item which involves *risk.* The risk may be emotional, spiritual or physical.

C. Put a "U" beside an item which you think others would think as *unconventional.*

D. Write an "F" next to any item which you think will *not* appear on your list in five years.

E. Put a ★ beside the *three most favorite* activities on your list.

(5) Get into groups of four and take two minutes each to talk about your list.

I AM LOVEABLE AND CAPABLE—IALAC

PURPOSE:

To help you to become more aware of the impact that actions and words have on others.

MATERIALS:

The *IALAC* Story; paper; pencil/pen.

PROCEDURE:

(1) Read the *IALAC* Story.

(2) Make a list in your *Notes to Myself* notebook of the people who have torn your *IALAC* sign during the past week. Be sure to note what behavior resulted in the tearing away.

(3) Now, make a list of the people whose *IALAC* sign you have torn in the past week. Also, record what behavior caused the tearing away.

(4) Finally, write five to eight suggestions you have on the following topic: "What Can be Done to Combat Sign-Tearing in our Society?"

(5) Share your suggestions with others in your class.

THE IALAC STORY

The letters *I-A-L-A-C* stand for *I Am Loveable And Capable*. People want to be seen by others as being loveable and capable. Many of our actions are reflections of this desire. The following story illustrates what happens to Jerry one day as he attempts to maintain his invisible *IALAC* sign:

Jerry's sleeping soundly when he is awakened by a pounding on the door. "Let's get moving, son. I can't afford for you to make me late to work again."

Jerry slowly sits up and rubs his eyes. As he thinks about the day ahead, he remembers that he hasn't done his research paper for English. "Oh well," he thinks, "I'll bet Mrs. Brantley doesn't expect me to hand it in anyway. She didn't want me to take her class in the first place."

Jerry gets dressed and goes down to breakfast. As he sits down, his mother says: "Please go put on another shirt. I can't believe you think that one looks right with those pants." Slowly, Jerry does what his mother requests.

As Jerry comes back down for breakfast, he hears his father starting the car. "Guess I'll be catching the bus," he thinks. Jerry climbs on the bus and looks for someone to sit with. Luckily, a new girl to school is sitting by herself and Jerry figures this is a good time to get acquainted. Just as he starts to sit by her, she puts her hand on the empty seat: "Sorry, but this is saved for someone else." Slowly, Jerry goes to the back of the bus.

At school, Jerry heads for Mrs. Louis' math class. He gets to her door just after the tardy bell rings. "Go to the Dean's office and get a note, Jerry. It's no wonder you don't understand what we are doing when you show up late. I'm tired of waiting on students like you who don't care about the future."

Jerry waits and waits in the Dean's office. Finally, he gets to see the Dean. By this time, his math class is over and he is late for P.E. They've already chosen sides, but one of the team captains yells: "You can be on their team, Jerry. We were stuck with you last week." Everyone laughs as Jerry joins the group.

Later in the day, as Jerry sits in his history class, he is handed a note from Mr. Pyle, the school counselor. His test scores are in the office and it is time to discuss them. Jerry doesn't know what to say or do as Mr. Pyle says: "Jerry, I think you'd better reconsider your plans to go to college. There is no way you'll get admitted with scores like these."

Finally, school is over for the day and Jerry heads for home. He walks in the door and asks his mother to give him a ride to the swimming pool. "I don't have time to run you everywhere in town. I'll sure be glad when you are old enough to drive and quit bugging me about taking you places."

At dinner, Jerry is informed that the family will be moving. His father has been offered a promotion and he has accepted the offer. When Jerry begins to say that he doesn't want to move, he is cut off by his dad's statement: "Look, we'll live where I say we'll live. This may be my last chance to make a good salary. Besides, you don't seem to have many friends here, anyway."

As Jerry climbs into bed that night, he looks at his torn and battered *IALAC* sign. Hopefully, tomorrow will be better. . . .

The above story is an adaptation of the original IALAC story by Dr. Sidney B. Simon.

Chapter III

I know that you believe you understand what you think I said, but I am not sure you realize that what you heard is not what I meant.

attentive listening

We hope that you're not planning to skip this chapter and take the art of listening for granted. Listening seems like an easy thing to do. Most of us spend a lot of our time listening — to television, radio, teachers, parents and friends. Some of you may be thinking: "I've been listening to people all my life, I don't need to learn more about listening — I need to learn how to get others to listen to me."

Listening is one of the most important skills that we can possess. Yet, often times it appears as if there are very few skilled listeners in today's world. Think about the various conversations that you have had today. While you were talking, how many people do you think really heard what you were trying to communicate? If they tried to tell others what you said and how you felt at the time, do you think they could describe accurately your ideas and feelings? Do they really know where you stand? Did they hear you or did they hear only what they wanted to hear?

What about your own listening habits? How involved do you get in a conversation? Do you understand others enough to state accurately their point of view? After a conversation is over, for example, do others leave feeling satisfied that you cared about what they had to say—that you understood them?

It often seems, at times, as though people aren't really interested in what we have to say, in what we believe to be important and in what we feel inside. Seldom do we get the opportunity to discuss our ideas in depth, because few people will take the time to listen and follow our thoughts for very long.

Sometimes people are so caught up in their own thoughts that they are not able to help us talk about our ideas in depth. In addition, many of the conversations we have are relatively "safe" ones. That is, we are not encouraged to explore our true beliefs, feelings and attitudes. Conversations with uninvolved people, talking only about superficial topics, appears to be the way the social game is played. But, it is one game that many find dissatisfying.

A facilitator of communication needs to be an active listener. When someone takes time and really listens to us, it is one of the most caring events we can experience. We all believe that our ideas are important and we want others to be interested in what we have to say. Those who listen carefully to what we are sharing can help validate our feelings of personal worth and add to our sense of well-being.

SIX STEPS FOR ATTENTIVE LISTENING

Let's look at what you can do to become a better listener. Here are a few simple suggestions that will help you to improve your skills.

I. FOCUS ON THE PERSON WHO IS TALKING.

You have probably heard how important it is to maintain a comfortable amount of eye contact with others while you are listening to them. But, there is more to listening than just eye contact. Listening requires a lot of mental energy because you are called upon to "block out" interfering noises, words, movements and even your own self-centered thoughts. People who talk with you must feel secure and sense that you are trying to understand them.

Have you ever found yourself daydreaming, or perhaps drifting off into your own thoughts, when you are attempting to listen to another person? If so, you are not alone. All too often we think about other things, or start planning how we are going to respond, instead of trying to fully understand the person's point of view. Sometimes we only hear part of what is being communicated and, thus, ideas may lose some of their meaning.

Attentive listeners avoid distorting ideas. They focus their attention upon general and specific ideas expressed. If you want to be a better listener, concentrate on the talker and keep a comfortable amount of eye contact.

2. BE AWARE OF THE FEELINGS OF THE TALKER.

Most people hear only the words being spoken and pay little attention to the *feelings* that are also communicated. Can you think of a time when you said one thing to a friend, but really were feeling another way? This frequently happens when people greet you with: "Hey, how are things going?"

Even though you might be feeling low, or maybe angry about something, you may find yourself saying: "Okay," or maybe, "Alright, everything is great!" Unless they really tune in to you and your feelings, they might assume that, indeed, everything is just fine. By disguising your feelings, they may never understand what you are experiencing.

Can you think of a time when you, or one of your friends, came home much later than expected? Perhaps what followed was something like what happened to Mark:

PARENT:

Where have you been? I can't believe that you've been out this late! What have you been doing?

MARK:

Well, after the show, we went to get something to eat and I forgot all about the time. I couldn't believe it when Chris told me what time it was.

PARENT:

You mean to tell me that you had no idea that it was this late? That's really hard for me to believe. Besides, it's your responsibility to be home on time. If I can't trust you, I guess you'll just have to not go out for awhile until you start being more trustworthy.

MARK:

You mean I can't go to the concert next weekend? That's not fair! I told you that we just lost track of the time. It won't happen again.

PARENT:

I know that it won't happen for awhile because you are not going anywhere. I'm tired of worrying about you while you are out half the night! What is there to do so late at night anyway? Until I can trust you to be home on time, you're not to make any plans after 7:00 p.m. Do you understand?

MARK:

I understand alright! You don't believe a word I say. Why is it that you always think I'm not telling you the truth? If you knew how late the other kids stay out, then you'd be glad that I'm home as early as this.

PARENT:

If you came home any later, you'd be in a lot more trouble than you are now. It doesn't matter to me what the other kids do, but I do expect you to do what I say. I'm tired of talking. Just remember that until further notice, you're not to go out of this house after 7:00 p.m.

While the preceding dialogue may not be the way your parents react when you come home late, it is a typical scene in many homes. Two of the feelings that many parents have when their son or daughter is out late are *fear* and *concern*. And yet, the words they use to express themselves primarily communicate *anger* and *distrust*. How very different the other part of the message is!

Professional counselors often use the word "empathy." It describes their attempt to understand the whole message being sent by the talker. It involves trying to see the world through the eyes of another person—to walk in that person's shoes. It is a difficult task to accomplish. This is especially true when someone expresses an opposite opinion.

3. DIFFERENTIATE BETWEEN UNPLEASANT AND PLEASANT FEELINGS.

When listening, *try to hear the feelings behind the words*. Ask yourself: "What else is the talker communicating?" One method that you might find helpful is to ask yourself: "Am I hearing *pleasant* feelings, *unpleasant* feelings or *both*?" Usually this will give you a hint as to what the talker is experiencing.

A list of the more common pleasant and unpleasant feeling words is presented in *Table I*. Review the list and familiarize yourself with as many words as you can. What other words would you add? Which ones do you use? Which of these sound strange to you?

Table I

UNPLEASANT FEELINGS WORDS

Abandoned	Distraught	Left Out	Sad
Agony	Disturbed	Lonely	Scared
Ambivalent	Dominated	Longing	Shocked
Angry	Divided	Low	Skeptical
Annoyed	Dubious	Mad	Sorrowful
Anxious	Empty	Maudlin	Startled
Betrayed	Envious	Mean	Strained
Bitter	Exasperated	Melancholy	Stupid
Bored	Exhausted	Miserable	Stunned
Burdened	Fatigued	Nervous	Tenuous
Cheated	Fearful	Odd	Tense
Cold	Flustered	Overwhelmed	Threatened
Condemned	Foolish	Pain	Tired
Confused	Frantic	Panicked	Trapped
Crushed	Frustrated	Persecuted	Troubled
Defeated	Frightened	Petrified	Uneasy
Despair	Grief	Pity	Unsettled
Destructive	Guilty	Pressured	Vulnerable
Different	Intimidated	Quarrelsome	Weak
Diminished	Irritated	Rejected	Weepy
Discontented	Isolated	Remorse	Worried
Distracted	Jealous	Restless	
	Jumpy		

PLEASANT FEELING WORDS

Adequate	Delighted	Generous	Loving
Affectionate	Determined	Glad	Loved
Befriended	Eager	Gratified	Peaceful
Bold	Ecstatic	Groovy	Pleasant
Calm	Enchanted	Happy	Pleased
Capable	Enhanced	Helpful	Proud
Caring	Energetic	High	Refreshed
Challenged	Enervated	Honored	Relaxed
Charmed	Enjoyed	Important	Relieved
Cheerful	Excited	Impressed	Rewarded
Clever	Fascinated	Infatuated	Safe
Comforting	Fearless	Inspired	Satisfied
Confident	Free	Joyful	Secure
Content	Fulfilled	Kind	Settled
			Sure
			Warm

It is important to feel some comfort with these feeling words. They will prove valuable when you get to the next chapter, which describes how to respond once you've heard the person.

Let's try an exercise:

1. Think about a *pleasant* experience you've had recently. Now, write down as many feeling words as you can that accurately describe that experience.

2. Think back to an *unpleasant* experience you have had recently. Write down the feeling words that come to mind as you recollect that event.

3. Now, write as many feeling words as you can that accurately describe how you are feeling *right now.*

Don't be too concerned if you found it difficult to write down feeling words for each of the situations. Perhaps the word lists in *Table I* will help.

Most people rarely talk about their feelings. Many have learned that it is safer and more socially acceptable to hide or ignore what they feel. Some years ago they were probably told not to be sensitive and aware of feelings. One indication of being a mature adult was: " Don't get too emotional!"

Over the years we have lost our ability to differentiate among feelings and have tended to rely on a few simple words, no matter what we are feeling. For example, when we say we are angry, we could also be feeling hurt, scared, uncomfortable, unsure or sad. And yet, we might only say that we are angry and not use the other feeling words that are also descriptive of what we are experiencing.

Try to expand your own *feeling-word vocabulary* so that you can respond more accurately and sensitively to what people say to you. Make a conscious effort to be more precise when expressing how you feel about a particular topic or situation. Be aware of the times when more than one feeling word is needed to clearly explain what you are experiencing.

Your feelings have a tremendous influence on your behavior. When you listen to what people are feeling, as well as what they are saying, you'll find yourself better able to understand and to accurately respond to them. They will feel more comfortable and relaxed when talking with you because you will be showing them, dramatically, that you are trying to understand how they see things.

4. SHOW THAT YOU UNDERSTAND WHAT IS BEING SAID.

Another way you can become an effective listener is to *periodically check out what you think you are hearing*. In checking, you are making a conscious effort to let the talker know that you are trying to understand. This process involves both the *content* (facts and events), as well as the *feelings* accompanying the content.

Here is an example of one listener, Steve, who checked to see if he understood what was being said:

TALKER:

You know, Steve, everytime I try to talk with Kim, it seems like she's bored with what I have to say. It's like she's doing me a favor by spending some of her PRECIOUS TIME with me.

STEVE:

You really find it frustrating—trying to get closer to Kim.

TALKER:

You said it! I really want to ask her out, but then I keep asking myself: "Why do I keep setting myself up for her to humiliate me?"

STEVE:

You're not really sure if it's worth it?

TALKER:

Yeah, I guess that's it. I'm just not sure if she and I would ever get along.

In this example, Steve used short empathic responses to see if he was on the right track. By doing this, he let the talker know that he was really listening and attempting to understand. This also gave the talker more assurance of being understood.

Can you think of a time when you talked to a friend, only to have your friend respond in such a way that it became evident that you were not understood? Few experiences can be as frustrating and irritating as spending time and energy with a careless and inattentive listener. It is very refreshing to find someone who listens and understands.

The following chapter will deal more specifically with the skill of responding. Be sure to read that chapter carefully. Your skill at responding will be the means by which you communicate to the talker that you are truly hearing and understanding . Listening and responding are two essential relationship-building skills, but attentive listening comes first.

5. BE A SELECTIVE LISTENER.

When most people talk, they usually have difficulty focusing on exactly what it is they want to say. Generally, there will be information, ideas or thoughts which are not as relevant or important as others. Thus, it is up to you to be a selective listener.

Use your skills and sensitivity to sort out the critical aspects of what is being said and unsaid. This enables the talker to stay "on task." Clarifying the main issues requires concentration and careful listening. Periodically, you might ask yourself: "What are the key points being expressed—which feelings are the most intense?"

It is often impossible—and usually not advisable—to respond to everything that a person says. Learning to be a selective listener will keep you "on target" and will assist you in choosing the most facilitative responses.

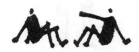

6. AVOID LABELING OR JUDGING THE TALKER.

A major barrier to hearing what a person is saying is the tendency to label and/or judge. Labeling and evaluating people usually prevents us from being able to "see the world from their point of view." Sensitivity is often decreased and our tendency is to think: "I already know what they are going to say." Thus, our efforts as listeners are greatly diminished.

Your own value system can greatly affect how you perceive the person who is talking and how well you will listen. Rather than thinking: "Do I agree or disagree?" or "Is this person a liberal or a conservative?", it might be more helpful and productive if you ask yourself: "How does this person feel? I wonder if I can learn how they came to hold those beliefs?"

The listener who wants to be facilitative hears the words and responds to the ideas that are communicated by focusing on the personal meaning that the talker gives to the spoken words. Being able to tempoarliy suspend your own judgments is an important part of being an effective listener. With practice and with awareness of how your own values affect your listening, you can learn to tune in to others better.

There are few things more important and special in this world than having someone whom you can depend upon to listen to you— someone who cares about what you have to say. You are going to have many opportunities this year to serve as a caring listener for your friends, your family and for those with whom you will work as a peer facilitator. You are going to be even more special and important to them than before.

Activity 3.1:
TWENTY QUESTIONS

PURPOSE:

To provide you with an opportunity to hear how others are dealing with various situations in their lives and to help you to develop the skill of asking questions.

MATERIALS:

None.

PROCEDURE:

(1) Pair up with another student—preferably someone with whom you seldom talk. Find a private place in the room.

(2) Take turns asking any two questions you choose. The questions may be general or personal.

The person being asked the question has the "right to pass" on any question. Continue taking turns (asking two questions, then answering two questions), until each has asked and answered ten questions.

(3) After all questions have been asked and answered, take one minute and summarize what you learned about your partner.

Activity 3.2:
ROGERIAN LISTENING

PURPOSE:

To develop a greater awareness of how involved and important the art of listening really is.

MATERIALS:

None

PROCEDURE:

(1) Put yourself into a group with two other persons. One person assumes the role of referee (monitor) while the other two people agree to be the talkers.

(2) Pick a topic of mutual interest on which the talkers have different points of view.

(3) The beginning talker has one minute in which to express views on a controversial topic. During this time, the referee and the other participant listen.

(4) Once the first talker stops, the second talker *must summarize the key statements made by the previous speaker* before offering a point of view. The role of the referee is to insure that *this accurate summarizing takes place before the second person continues.*

(5) The two talkers continue to exchange points of view (after summarizing the previous statements of the other) until they agree that each understands the viewpoint of the other.

(6) The referee now changes place with one of the talkers. A new topic is chosen and the process continues.

(7) Write a short summary in your *Notes to Myself* notebook concerning your reactions to this activity.

Activity 3.3:

HOW I SEE THE WORLD

PURPOSE:

To share ideas about the world and practice listening for pleasant and unpleasant feelings.

MATERIALS:

A large piece of paper that can first be cut into a circle and then into parts; pencils, magic markers or crayons.

PROCEDURE:

(1) Form a group with three or four other members of the class.

(2) The large piece of paper represents the world. Cut the paper into parts. Each person is given a part of the "world."

(3) On your portion of "the world," draw some symbols or pictures that represent some of your thoughts about how you see the world today.

(4) After the group has recorded their thoughts, all of the individuals, in turn, tell the group the meaning of their pictures.

(5) While each person is talking, the other group members listen for feelings—unpleasant and pleasant.

(6) After each person has finished, the group tries to remember the feelings that were shared. A list of these feeling words is made.

(7) After everyone has had a turn, look at the total list of pleasant and unpleasant words. Discuss your reactions.

Chapter IV

A friend is one who knows you as you are, understands where you have been, accepts who you've become and still invites you to grow.

the facilitative responses

It is not enough for a facilitator to be a "nice person." Even though we enjoy being around people who are friendly and interesting, something more is needed if they are to facilitate our personal growth and development. As suggested earlier, there are certain conditions or characteristics that are essential in the helping process (i.e. accepting, understanding, caring and genuineness). These conditions may be a usual part of one's personality style or they can be created through the interaction that takes place.

A skilled facilitator increases the chance that the helping conditions will be present and that the relationship will be beneficial. The important question is: "What can you do that will create these helping conditions?" In this chapter we will attempt to answer that question.

BEING A FACILITATOR: ART OR SCIENCE?

Being a facilitator might be viewed as both an art *and* a science. We know that the helping process can be improved through the use of special skills and methods that have been identified through scientific investigations. While these skills and methods are valuable, knowledge of them alone does not seem to be enough.

The artistic part of helping refers to the intuitive elements or emotional aspects of the process. In the art of helping a person, the facilitator develops a feel for the relationship. Sometimes people call it common sense or good judgment. The helper senses the important ingredients of the process and is "tuned in." But, even the most sensitive and intuitive persons can be assisted to be better facilitators when they use the information and theory that has developed from the work of social and behavorial scientists.

Counselors and human service workers, for example, are highly skilled and have a professional background that enables them to work with many kinds of people. These specialists have acquired detailed skills and knowledge through years of hard work, study, research and practice. While we will always need such specialists in the helping professions—and value their contributions—there is evidence that others, with less experience and formal training, can also facilitate others toward more personal growth. This seems particularly true when these less trained people work with a specialist—working together in the helping process.

Being a facilitator is not a matter of knowing what techniques to use. In fact, the word "technique" is sometimes met with skepticism because it can imply that someone is deliberately and consciously trying to manipulate somebody else. When skills are forced, they are no longer helpful. On the other hand, when the skills are a genuine part of the helping process and used with care, they can help communicate the facilitator's attitude of acceptance, respect, interest, positive regard and so forth.

When they are used to communicate the facilitator's understanding and to help someone explore a problem, then they are considered facilitative. When they drift into becoming gimmicks in which a person is tricked into making a decision or deceived into feeling safe—when in fact that is not the case—then the use of such skills may even be harmful.

Learning a skill in interpersonal communication is no different than perfecting a skill in a sport. For example, when people are first learning to swim, it is helpful to know about certain movements that will coordinate their arms, hands and legs, as well as the breathing process. To simply throw them into the water and say: "Sink or swim!" is not the easiest way to teach swimming, although it has been suggested as one method. Being thrown into the water, without some preliminary skills, usually causes people to thrash around, panic, struggle unnecessarily and exert a lot of excess energy. That person would probably become more cautious about getting into the water the next time around. Very few would find this particular method effective.

Most of us would prefer to work closely with a coach who has analyzed and understands the sport of swimming. This coach understands the principles and the basic skills that will help us learn to enjoy swimming. With the help of a coach, the skill of swimming can help us survive in the water and it can be enjoyable. Breaking down the process, analyzing it, identifying the important components and then selecting those to work on is the job of the coach.

In this sense, you are going to be coached in the art of being a facilitator. You, too, will have an opportunity to practice the more detailed skills that, when combined, will make you an effective helper.

Before we go any further, let's look at some special situations. The following might have occurred in your school. Each situation is described briefly, followed by some possible responses that you could make. Imagine that you are trying to help.

Read over the responses and *rank them in order from one to six, beginning with the one you consider to be the least understanding and helpful (No.1)*. The wording of the response may not be exactly what you would use, but choose a response that is close to the type that you would tend to favor.

Situation 1

John is a new student to the school. One day you start a conversation with him and he surprises you when he says: "I like it okay, but I don't seem to have any friends here and I can't figure it out. I had a lot of friends at the other school, but here. . . ."

_____(A) Well, John, you'll get around more and get more friends pretty soon. You're still new here.

_____(B) Hey, look, John, if you want to have more friends, then you've got to get more involved with some of the school's activities—just do your thing.

_____(C) What have you been doing to make friends?

_____(D) You're saying that you had more friends before you came here and you're not sure why you don't have more now.

_____(E) You're feeling left out and wondering what you can do about it.

_____(F) Well, maybe one reason you haven't as many friends here is that you don't have confidence in yourself and you're holding back.

Situation 2

Sue is studying in the library. She feels pressed to get assignments done, but her girlfriends use her table to group around. They talk about events around the school. Later, she says to you: "I really like the girls, but the trouble is that they are stopping by to talk so much that I'm not getting my assignments done. I don't want to be unfriendly and tell them to go away, but I don't want to flunk this work either."

_____(A) In time you will find a happy medium between studying and having a social life, Sue.

_____(B) You have to learn to take a stand, Sue. Assert yourself. Tell them you're busy when you have to study.

_____(C) You want to talk with them, but not when you're in the library doing your assignments.

_____(D) You must not feel very secure about your friendships with them, if you can't tell them to leave you alone and let you finish your work.

_____(E) How often do they stop by and talk?

_____(F) It's frustrating knowing you want to finish your work, but also be involved with your friends.

Situation 3

Janna says: "I don't like the way our discussion group is going. We don't seem to accomplish anything. I've got so much to do and a lot better ways to spend my time."

_____(A) *What do you think these meetings should accomplish, Janna?*

_____(B) *It would help, Janna, if you would tell us what you're feeling. You need to contribute more if we are going to get things done.*

_____(C) *If I follow you, Janna, you think that these meetings are a waste of your time.*

_____(D) *You are disappointed with our meetings, especially with what we are accomplishing.*

_____(E) *Once we get rolling here, Janna, you'll like what's happening. We just need some more time.*

_____(F) *Because you don't like the way things are going, you're thinking of other things besides being here.*

Situation 4

Harold says: "I think I'd like to go to college next year, but then maybe the military service would give me the same thing. College would be a lot more fun and I'd be with my friends, but then the military would pay for my education and I'd get to travel. Regardless, it's going to be great!"

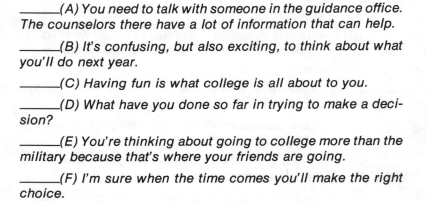

_____(A) You need to talk with someone in the guidance office. The counselors there have a lot of information that can help.

_____(B) It's confusing, but also exciting, to think about what you'll do next year.

_____(C) Having fun is what college is all about to you.

_____(D) What have you done so far in trying to make a decision?

_____(E) You're thinking about going to college more than the military because that's where your friends are going.

_____(F) I'm sure when the time comes you'll make the right choice.

What a facilitator says in a conversation is very important. Every response makes an impact. As the interaction between the facilitator and the person being helped continues, more responses are made and this affects their relationship and their perceptions. If the helpee gains a favorable impression of the facilitator, there is a better chance that a helping relationship will develop and that the person can be assisted. Therefore, it is most important for us to understand the probable impact that different responses have on most individuals.

THE HIGH AND LOW FACILITATIVE RESPONSES

Studies of verbal behavior in counseling, psychotherapy and teaching indicate that there are many kinds of responses. Some are more helpful than others and can be categorized from the least to the most facilitative. Here are six categories of responses that can help you be more organized and systematic in your efforts:

1. *Advising and Evaluating*
2. *Analyzing and Interpreting*
3. *Reassuring and Supporting*
4. *Questioning and Probing*
5. *Clarifying and Summarizing Events*
6. *Reflecting and Understanding Feelings*

All of these responses, at one time or another, might be facilitative. No single response can be classified as either good or bad or effective or ineffective. Rather, we must consider the situation, the timing and the probable effect that it has. We do know, however, that *some responses tend to be more facilitative than others in building a helping relationship.*

Let's look now at the responses which you selected in the preceding situations. Remember, you wanted to select a response that would enable the person to view you as caring and understanding.

The six responses are placed in order of the *least* facilitative (1) to the *most* facilitative (6) and are shown in *Table II*.

Check your answers with the table. Using *Table II*, you can see how each of the six responses in the different situations are classified. If, for example, you tended to favor C, D and E in the first situation (though not necessarily in that order), then you were selecting the *most* facilitative responses. On the other hand, if you selected A, B and F, you were favoring the *low* facilitative responses.

You are probably wondering: "How do I know when a statement is rated as a high facilitative response? Why are some more effective than others?" Let's see if we can get a better understanding of these responses and how they can be helpful in our relationships with others.

Table II
FACILITATIVE RESPONSES

CASE SITUATIONS	1. ADVISING or EVALUATING	2. INTERPRETING or ANALYZING	3. REASSURING or SUPPORTING	4. QUESTIONING	5. CLARIFYING or SUMMARIZING	6. REFLECTING or UNDERSTANDING
Situation 1 (John)	B	F	A	C	D	E
Situation 2 (Sue)	B	D	A	E	C	F
Situation 3 (Janna)	C	F	E	A	B	D
Situation 4 (Harold)	A	E	F	D	C	B

LEAST FACILITATIVE - - - - - MOST FACILITATIVE

I. ADVISING AND EVALUATING

Giving advice is one of the most popular responses that we make when trying to help others. Perhaps this is because we usually receive some kind of suggestion when we let others know that we are having a problem.

Think about a time when you had a problem and looked for someone to talk with. Did you seek them out for help in understanding your problem better or were you hoping that they would give you some advice? More often than not, you wanted your story to be heard. But, most people cannot wait to hear the story and they tend to rush in with advice. Too often our parents and teachers tend to judge and evaluate a situation and, then, quickly make a suggestion. However, advice is not always helpful, even though it may be a good solution to the problem. When it is threatening, the response produces some hesitation, resistence, and indecisiveness, preventing us from exploring the situation.

An advising or evaluating response implies what you *might or ought to do*. Here are some examples:

Don't quit school, you can get a better job if you graduate.

What you need to do is try to understand your teacher's point of view instead of arguing.

If you would study more, then you would get better grades.

If I were you, I'd take a more positive approach to the situation and try to do better next time around.

You need to find some time alone where you can do your home-work and not be disturbed.

If you don't start getting good grades, you're not going to be able to go to college.

You're being unfair in your criticism of Mr James. You should get to know him better.

Get started early on your term paper and don't put it off like you usually do.

Advice tells another person how to behave or what to do. Advice is cheap and most people are willing to give it. You will also note, as seen in some of the previous statements, that advice can be a *projection* of our needs, problems or values. That is, we may begin to tell you how we would solve the problem if we were in your shoes.

For example, the statement: "If I were you. . ." emphasizes how advice can come from our own experiences, rather than waiting to find out what the problem is all about. Notice how the following lead-in phrases are designed to tell people what they should do:

One good way is. . . .

Why don't you. . . .

You should. . . .

I think. . . .

What you need is. . . .

You ought to. . . .

If I were you. . . .

The thing to do is. . . .

If you don't, . . . then. . . .

Don't you think. . . .

In other words, many people think of the problem as their own and the desire to give advice is aroused. It is difficult to be objective when giving advice. That is one reason why it tends to be a low facilitative response. When advice is relevant, logical and practical, it can make sense. But if the advice is untimely, and if it is viewed as a simple solution to a difficult problem, it may be dismissed as useless. Most important, advice can keep people from taking responsibility for their own decisions.

People should have an opportunity to be responsible for their own decisions. There is a lot of satisfaction in resolving problems. When we are given advice and depend on it, there is a growing feeling that we are not responsible for ourselves and that we are not capable of making decisions. When others seem so capable in giving advice by making the solution sound so easy, we may begin to feel inadequate. This feeling of inadequacy creates more anxiety and defensiveness. Thus, advice with this kind of impact is not facilitative and may even be harmful.

Evaluation also makes us think defensive. This is true even when it is positive. When people evaluate our work, there is a tendency to think some of the following thoughts:

They think that I am. . . .

They want me to. . . .

They probably won't take it as if I. . . .

They probably won't like it if I. . . .

I guess that means that they are. . . and I am. . . .

Some parents and teachers use advice and evaluation in an attempt to encourage us to do something. When praise (evaluation), for example, is used to motivate, there is a tendency for us to believe that certain expectations must be met before we are of value. To continue to "produce for others" in order to gain love and attention can be self-defeating.

Still another problem of evaluating or giving advice is that it is often viewed as coming from a position of authority. The advice-giver assumes a role of superiority while the receiver "looks up" to the expert. When a person is having a problem, that person doesn't want to feel inferior or talked down to.

This is not to say that advice or evaluation should never be used. No doubt we have all benefited from some good advice at one time or another. *When advice is timely and relevant to a situation, it has great impact and can be very helpful.*

Unfortunately, we tend to rush in with advice while attempting to "fix people up." We are too quick to give advice and it is often given without fully understanding the situation. Sadly enough, advice often comes from generalizations and, even if it makes good sense, the major message to the other person is that we do not understand, nor do we care, to take the time to understand. Rather, we assume the problem is typical of others and, therefore, a little advice will help.

To avoid giving non-facilitative advice, slow yourself down and don't rush in. You might first think to yourself: "I know what might be done, but I wonder if they will come to the same idea through exploring the situation more;" or "I know what I would do, but maybe if I help them examine the ideas and clarify the situation, they might come up with the same solution— or maybe a better one."

It is much easier to give advice than it is to give of our time and get involved with another person's problems and conflicts. Giving advice is expedient and, at first glance, it makes us think that we are moving things along. Perhaps that is why it is so prevalent in our society. It's quick, fast and easy, but many times it's not very facilitative.

Effective facilitators value the ideas of others and try to understand the meaning and importance of them. They avoid labeling us (e.g. "snob," "weird," "negative," "stupid," "crybaby," "lazy"). They try to avoid statements that begin with: "Well, I think you should. . ." or "What you need to do is. . . ." They know that there is a place for advice and evaluation, but that it is important to restrain early advice and evaluation in an attempt to find the most appropriate solution. Even though they tend to be the more popular responses, advice and evaluation have limited value.

If you still are not sure about the impact that advice or evaluation can have upon a person, why not try it out with someone? Give someone some "good advice," or at least what you hope will be good advice, and then notice their reaction. Most likely the person's first reaction will be something like: "Yes, but. . ." or "That's not a bad idea, however. . . ." No matter how you look at it, advice and evaluation must be rated as low facilitators of communcation. Although they can be helpful at times, they are not the most effective responses.

2. ANALYZING AND INTERPRETING

Some people think that they can be a helper by analyzing the situation for another person. Analyzing and interpreting responses probably gained their popularity from early counseling theories. Too many times we have seen old movies where the counselor/therapist is attempting to analyze the situation, trying to tell persons why they are doing the things they are doing. It's an attempt to look at some deep hidden reason that makes people do the things they do. Consider these statements:

Don't you see, one of the reasons you want to quit school is because you want others to feel sorry for you and tell you how important they think you are.

The reason you don't talk in class is that you are afraid that you're going to make a mistake and be criticized.

You are unhappy because you don't have a girlfriend.

You walked away from our group because you thought we were talking about you.

You are just saying that because you don't like to do those things and you're afraid to try.

In each of these examples, there is an attempt to explain, analyze or interpret someone's behavior. There is an attempt to give the person some additional insight by connecting one event to another. In trying to explain, or give insight, the interpretive responses suggest *what the person might or ought to think*. This often makes people defensive. It discourages them from revealing more ideas for fear that these ideas might also be interpreted or explained away.

Most of us don't like having others know more about ourselves than we do. When someone tries to analyze or interpret our behavior, that is exactly what they are saying: "I know more about you than you do about yourself."

One problem with analyzing or interpreting behavior is that the interpretation usually comes from a generalization about people. We frequently think that because we have studied other people, we now have some idea as to why certain behavior occurs. The problem, of course, is that none of us like to be seen as a typical textbook case. We like to be viewed as unique. What was true for somebody else may not be true for us.

If you want to be facilitative, you will probably try to avoid such statements as: "Ah, ha! I know what your problem is;" or "The reason you don't like. . . is because. . . ." Instead, you will want to help people think about themselves and their feelings, rather than guessing what causes them to do the things they do. It is a much safer approach because you do not have to be an "expert" in human behavior.

It is not your task to have studied numerous similar cases and to be able to make a diagnosis. On the contrary, you will be much more effective when you avoid analyzing or interpreting.

3. REASSURING AND SUPPORTING

It is nice to have support. It feels good to be reassured, especially at times when our self-confidence is beginning to waiver a little. Like the other responses, reassuring and supporting statements can be helpful, providing that we do not rush in with them. *Reassuring or supporting type statements suggest that a person need not feel a certain way.* When we rush in with support and reassurance, we deny the feeling that is there. We imply that the feeling is normal and so common that the person need not be concerned. Look at these examples:

Everyone feels like that at one time or another.

It may look bad now, but everything is going to turn out alright.

My mother is like that too.

That happened to me once and before long it just went away.

You remind me a lot of Jane. She had similar problems, but as she grew older, the problems didn't seem so big.

You always say you're worried about passing exams, but you do okay each time.

I know how you feel.

Interestingly enough, reassuring or supporting statments are the second most popular responses used by teachers and parents when they are trying to be understanding. Only advice and evaluation are used more frequently. Why are such statements so popular?

In most cases, people report that they are trying to build self-confidence, to encourage a person to do better. Yet, when the statement has been studied in terms of its impact, the result is less than expected. The real message that comes through is: "You should not feel as you do." Rather than communicate acceptance, respect or understanding, it treats the person's feelings as of little importance.

Have you heard statements similar to the following:

It's always dark, just before the sun shines.

We cannot direct the wind, but we can adjust our sails.

Things will be better tomorrow.

Remember, each dawn is a new beginning.

Nobody's perfect.

Things take time.

Well, people are only human.

These philosophical truisms or Pollyanna-like statements are often intended as offering encouragement, hope and security, but they frequently communicate a lack of interest or understanding. While reassuring or supporting statements can make a person feel good at first, later, the real impact sets in and there is a feeling of being misunderstood. Thus, the conclusion: "Hey, you really didn't understand me—you just wanted to get rid of me."

4. QUESTIONING AND PROBING

Questioning is an important skill. Too many times, however, we ask questions when other kinds of statements might be made. Bombarding people with a lot of questions can make them feel defensive and uneasy. They wonder why they don't have the answers.

A question seems simple enough. It is designed to obtain additional information, provoke thought or encourage discussion. It implies that it would be beneficial to discuss the situation in more detail and it helps to focus the discussion. Questions not only determine the kind of information collected and the extent of that information, but, most importantly, they determine the direction of a relationship.

Let's suppose you want to talk to someone about a problem. If you initiate the helping relationship through a long series of questions, you might be perceived as a person who is going to provide a solution. Why did you ask your questions? Did you hope the questions would help the person gain insight? Or, did you really plan to provide a solution?

Questions can stimulate discussion. They can be an important part of any interpersonal relationship. But, there are certain things that should be kept in mind when posing questions:

1. What is the *purpose* of the question and what is the *assumption* behind that question?

2. Are you trying to get more information? Do you want the person to *elaborate*?

3. Is there an *alternative response* that can be just as effective?

4. What *impact* is the question going to have on your relationship?

Let's take a look at some kinds of questions that can be asked.

The "open and closed" questions.

Questions can be categorized as "open or closed." The *open question* encourages the person to develop an answer and talk at greater length and in more detail. The *closed question* usually calls for a simple "yes" or "no" and it is typically phrased so that the answers are limited to a few words.

Note the following examples:

Do you get along with your teachers? (closed)

What can you tell me about your teachers? (open)

Do you like school? (closed)

How do you feel about school? (open)

Is your plan to start all over again? (closed)

What are your plans at this point? (open)

An examination of these questions can be valuable, especially when you want to obtain some specific information. They can help clarify a situation quickly. But, the open-ended question encourages the person to share more personal feelings and thoughts. In that sense, it is more facilitative.

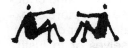

The "why" question.

Most people don't know the reasons they do the things they do. Yet, they often are asked: "Why did you do that? Do you know why you do the things you do? Why do you like a particular food? Why don't you play a particular sport? Do you know why you get the grades you do?"

The answers to these and similar questions are complicated. We are not always sure of the answers, but if a why question is posed to us, we usually try to give some explanation.

It is doubtful that we will ever understand or discover all the reasons why we do the things we do. To encourage people to give us a rational explanation of their behavior may not be productive. For this reason, many facilitators try to limit their use of the why question. They know that it makes people defensive and forces them to justify their behavior.

The why question also has become infamous because it is frequently not intended as a question. Rather, it is used to indicate disapproval or displeasure. For example:

Why don't you cut your hair?

Why do you wear those old clothes?

Why don't you study more?

Why are you late to class?

Why didn't you do your homework?

While these questions may be legitimate, and the people asking them may really want us to give the information requested, more often than not they are really saying: "Study more; Don't be late; Complete your work;" and so forth.

We have learned that *the why question is frequently viewed as advice and many times as criticism.* Because advice and criticism tend to threaten people, they feel less free to explore or examine the reasons that led them to a particular act or decision. Instead of forcing people to explain themselves or to justify their positions, it might be more appropriate to focus on *what*, *where*, *when*, *how* and *who*.

The "what, where when, how and who" questions.

The *what, where, when, how* and *who* words, when used in questions, enable the respondent to be more specific and precise. They are less threatening and more revealing.

For instance, instead of asking: "Why do you smoke?", a better question might be: "What makes you want to smoke?" Instead of asking: "Why don't you like school?", a better question might be: "What is it about school that you don't like?" It is possible that people responding to these questions might gain more insight and look at some aspects of their lives that might be influencing them.

Obviously, the way in which a question is phrased can have a definite effect on both the answer and the relationship. When a question comm) unciates that you are really interested, that you care and that you want to understand, then it is facilitative. At times, however, in your eagerness to help people, you may fall into the trap of asking too many questions. It is easy to ask questions, but they too are limiting. They imply that you are interested, but they do not communicate, necessarily, that you are understanding.

Turning questions into statements.

When you find yourself asking too many questions, you might try turning them into statements. A reflective statement, for example, encourages the person to keep talking. It doesn't interrupt the flow of communication, because it doesn't call for an answer. It focuses on clarifying and summarizing ideas. For instance:

Closed Question:

Do you like playing football?

Statement:

You really like playing football.

Open Question:

What happened to your hair?

Statement:

I'm surprised that you changed hairstyles.

5. CLARIFYING AND SUMMARIZING EVENTS

Clarifying or summarizing responses attempt to identify the most significant ideas emerging in the conversation. They are usually made in two situations. First, they might be helpful when there is some doubt as to whether you are really understanding people's thoughts and feelings. In this case a clarification statement simply checks out what you have been hearing. For example: "Let me see if I am following you. You said. . . ."

In the second situation the clarification or summary statement is used deliberately because you want to help people hear what they have said. They may want to correct themselves or confirm the statement, but it gives them an opportunity to hear their thoughts aloud.

The clarifying statement involves the use of fresh words and simplifies what has been said. It emphasizes the ideas, events or content of the discussion.

Look at these examples of beginning a clarifying statement:

You seem to be saying that. . . .

If I hear you correctly, you're saying. . . .

If I'm following you, you're telling me that. . . .

Correct me if I'm wrong, but you're thinking that. . . .

Let me see if I understand what you have been saying. You said. . . .

Let's see, your aim is to. . . .

In other words, you're trying to. . . .

Out of all the things that you've said, what seems to be coming out is. . . .

From what you've said, it seems that. . . .

Clarifying statements not only check out where people are during a discussion, but they reassure them that you are following their ideas and are trying to understand them.

A summary statement focuses on those things that have impressed you most and that you want to highlight. For example, here are some phrases that indicate a summarization of ideas:

Let's see now, at this point you've said. . . and. . . and. . . .

From what you've been saying, I've heard three things. First, . . . second, . . . and third. . . .

You've mentioned at least two possible solutions. One was. . . and the second was. . . .

When you listen to people talk, you will note that they usually express several thoughts and feelings at the same time. Some people may ramble in their excitement to share ideas with you.

As a facilitator, you can be helpful by summarizing some of the ideas. There is a tendency, however, for most people to focus on the last idea that was presented. That is, if a person expresses four different ideas while talking, the listener will tend to respond only to the fourth idea. An effective facilitator, however, will be able to respond to any or all four of the ideas.

6. REFLECTING AND UNDERSTANDING FEELINGS

Perhaps the most facilitative response is one in which we convey that we are reading a person's feelings. Yet, the reflecting or understanding feeling response is seldom used in the classroom or in the home. For example, observations indicate that less than one out of a thousand times will a feeling response be made in a typical classroom. Look at these responses:

You are feeling disappointed, Joan.

You're irritated right now and you don't feel like being part of the group.

You're tired and wondering what we are going to do next.

The reflecting or understanding of feelings statement is perhaps the most difficult to learn. You must be an empathic listener. In order to be empathic, you have to go beyond the ideas that are expressed to the feelings that accompany the words. *You not only hear what a person is literally talking about, but you also hear the feelings. It is these feelings that you reflect to the person.*

Reflecting feelings involves more than a simple restatement of words. It is not a case of paraphrasing. In that sense, it should not be confused with clarifying or summarizing. *Clarifying and summarizing statements emphasize ideas or events.* Nor should a reflection of feelings be confused with interpretation, which tends to emphasize the reason a person is feeling or acting a certain way. The reflecting or understanding of feelings response *"echos the feeling that may not have been expressed openly, but was clearly a part of the response."*

To begin a sentence with *"you feel"* does not necessarily mean that you are reflecting a person's feelings. For instance: "I feel you would make a good class president" is not a feeling-oriented response. It is an *opinion*. There are no feeling words in the statement and the focus is on the opinion-giver.

It might be helpful if you ask yourself: "How would I feel if I were to say something like that?" or "How would I have to feel to do something like that?" After answering these questions, you might have some additional insight as to what the person is feeling. The problem with this approach to understanding, however, is that we often *project* our own feelings on others. We assume that if we feel that way, then others do too. This may not be the case.

A person cannot talk or behave without showing feeling. All of us feel something at all times. Both our verbal and nonverbal behavior reveal these feelings.

In Chapter 3, you learned that it can be helpful to listen for unpleasant and/or pleasant feelings. This technique is especially valuable when you are trying to reflect feelings. *First, tune in to the person's feeling. Then, put that feeling word into your statement.* For example:

"Being a peer facilitator looks like a lot of fun, but I also hear that it can be hard work. I don't know whether to be one or not."

What were the feeling words? If you identified curiosity and un-certainty, you might be able to say something like this:

"You are curious about the program," or *"You are not certain if the program is for you."*

There may be other feelings present too. Depending on the tone of voice, look of the eyes, body position and so forth, the person might reveal some *unspoken feelings* to which you could re-spond.

Nonverbal communication is always taking place between a facilitator and the person who is being helped. Nonverbal communication is not mentioned in most texts about counseling. We need to learn more about it. We recognize its importance and sense that it is a powerful means of communicating.

Nonverbal communication emphasizes our tone of voice, the speed at which we speak, the pauses and the hesitations. It includes stammering, stuttering and stumbling, as well as other vocal expressions of emotion. It reminds us that our facial expressions, gestures and other parts of our body convey meaning. While body language has become an important area of study, there is no reliable dictionary that analyzes and defines this language. Therefore, we should be cautious in trying to interpret nonverbal behavior. We can be misled easily by dress, appearance, gestures or facial expressions. While these are important to the total context of what a person is thinking and feeling, they should not be isolated and viewed as symbols of what a person believes and thinks.

A reflecting or understanding of feelings response has a lot of power. There is no need to immediately follow such a statement with another statement. Let the impact of the reflection rest. Pause. Give the person an opportunity to hear your statement. It can be a pleasant experience for both of you. Usually the person will nod positively and continue to talk more.

It is possible that your reflection of feelings could be rejected, even though you believe you are accurate. Sometimes responding accurately to feelings can be a little frightening. Some people, for instance, become uneasy when they realize that they are revealing so much of themselves. This is especially true when they are insecure, cautious and doubtful of others.

Interestingly enough, however, attempts at reflecting feelings are likely to be facilitative because they emphasize your intent to be understanding.

Learning to tune in to feelings and reflecting them accurately takes a lot of practice. It does not come easy. There have not been many adult models to provide good examples to growing children. Trained counselors and psychotherapists work many hours to learn this skill in order that they can communicate more effectively with their clients.

For many years our society did not encourage the disclosure of feelings. Feelings were viewed as being private. There are still some people today who think that a person's feelings should rarely be discussed. Some try to disown them, to deny them or to distort them for fear that they would reveal some kind of character weakness. For too many years the pattern in our society has been to encourage relationships that are distant, formal and lacking in personal understanding. Subsequently, many of our problems today are caused by a lack of under-standing— a lack of feeling.

Hiding our feelings is a step on the road to personal dysfunc-tioning and "emotional disturbance." We need a society that humanizes people and that encourages caring relationships. *We need you to help facilitate others and create the helping conditions.*

Activity 4.1:

LEARNING TO BE FACILITATIVE (TRIADS)

PURPOSE:

To give you an opportunity to practice using the facilitative responses outlined in this chapter.

MATERIALS:

The Facilitator's Report Card, pencil/pen.

PROCEDURE:

(1) With two other people, form a group (triads). Number off: 1, 2 and 3. Let No. 1 be the talker, No. 2 the facilitator and No. 3 the observer.

(2) The talker begins by speaking to the facilitator for three minutes, while the observer watches and takes notes. The talker is to speak on: "Something I Would Like to Change About Myself."

The facilitator assists the talker by responding with high facilitative responses—*reflecting feelings, clarifying ideas* and *asking open-ended questions.* Remember, no advice, no praise and *no interpretations.* Follow the lead of the talker.

The observer watches the facilitator and records observations by marking on the *Facilitator's Report Card.* After three minutes, the observer—using the report card—tells the facilitator what seemed to be happening (about two minutes is allowed for this part).

(3) Now, the same talker, facilitator and observer go through another three minute round. This time the talker speaks about "Something I Like About Myself," while the facilitator and observer repeat their same roles. Again, after three minutes, the observer gives a report.

(4) Switch roles in a second and third round (with the same talking assignments) until all three have been in each role.

(5) After each person has been in all three roles, discuss among yourselves: "How I Felt About Doing This Experience."

DISCUSSION QUESTIONS:

Here are some discussion questions and comments that might be helpful:

How is what you dislike (or like) about yourself related to your school life? family life? hopes for the future?

For discussion afterwards:

How do you feel when talking about yourself?

Which part did you like best?

Was it easier to talk about the negative or positive aspect of yourself?

Which aspect was the easiest to facilitate?

What did you learn from this experience?

THE FACILITATOR'S REPORT CARD

(Check or Tally)

1.	Evaluated and gave advice	Yes	No	Not Sure
2.	Interpreted or analyzed	Yes	No	Not Sure
3.	Used questions:			
	Open	Yes	No	Not Sure
	Closed	Yes	No	Not Sure
4.	Responded to feelings	Yes	No	Not Sure
5.	Clarified or summarized	Yes	No	Not Sure
6.	Supported or reassured	Yes	No	Not Sure
7.	Had good eye contact	Yes	No	Not Sure
8.	Seemed at ease	Yes	No	Not Sure
9.	Was able to keep the talker speaking on the subject	Yes	No	Not Sure
10.	Seemed to be an effective listener	Yes	No	Not Sure

Activity 4.2:
LET ME HELP

PURPOSE:

To provide you with a personal experience related to the effects of using low rather than high facilitative responses.

MATERIALS:

None.

PROCEDURE:

(1) Get a partner.

(2) Each of you think of your response to the following question: "What is one decision you are trying to make right now?" It may be a major or a minor decision. The only criterion is that it must be a real situation and you aren't sure what you should do.

(3) Decide who will be the talker and who will be the listener. The *talker* has two minutes to share the decision being contemplated. The *listener's* role is to use only the three *lowest* facilitative responses: advice, analysis and reassurance in attempting to assist the talker.

(4) After two minutes, reverse roles. The new listener once again uses only the *low* facilitative responses. Continue for two minutes.

(5) Each of you have had an opportunity to talk about your decision to a person using *low* facilitative responses. Now, take another two minutes to talk about your decision. This time the facilitator will use only *high* facilitative responses (open-ended questions, clarifying and summarizing and reflecting feelings).

(6) Share your reactions to this activity with the rest of the class.

Activity 4.3:
THE OPPOSITE SEX

PURPOSE:

To practice listening, clarifiying and responding to feelings. To learn about the thoughts and feelings of the opposite sex.

MATERIALS:

Chairs for an inner and outer circle arrangement.

PROCEDURE:

(1) Form two circles—one inside the other.

(2) All the boys sit in the inside circle while the girls occupy the outside chairs.

(3) As the girls listen (no comments), the boys talk about:

    A. What do you think it would be like to be a girl?

    B. What are the advantages?

    C. What are the disadvantages?

    D. The problems?

(4) After eight to ten minutes, from the girls' group should come:

    A. Four clarifying responses

    B. Four feeling responses

    C. Two questions

    D. One piece of advice or interpretation

The girls' responses should be related directly to what the boys have said.

(5) Now, change places—girls on the inside and the boys on the outside.

(6) Repeat the same procedures as above (3). This time the boys listen (without comment) while the girls discuss what it would be like to be a boy.

(7) The boys then respond as outlined in (4).

(8) Use the remainder of the time for open discussion.

Chapter V

I like being with you.
Sometimes it hurts to tell it like it is.

facilitative feedback : praising and confronting

We have emphasized the use of high facilitative responses. We have stressed the importance of being seen as a caring person, one who is understanding, accepting and genuine. This encourages people with whom we are working to feel more secure and to self-disclose more.

But now, maybe you are asking the question: "What about *my* feelings? Am I always *just a listener? When do I share some of my feelings and ideas?"*

A helping relationship cannot be one-sided. If you are only listening and reflecting ideas and feelings, people will soon grow tired of your behavior. Most people will want to know more about you and your thoughts about them. They want *feedback* from you.

We learn who we are by the reactions other people have to us. We have been greatly influenced by our parents, friends and neighbors through what they say and do in our presence. Sometimes their thoughts and feelings about us are clear, while, at other times, we have to guess or read between the lines. When they are clear, it helps answer the question: "Who am I?" When they are fuzzy or imprecise, it confuses us and tends to make us cautious in our relationships.

Behavior is influenced by consequences. For instance, if you tell a funny story and people laugh, then you might begin to think of yourself as a good story teller. On the other hand, if people fail to laugh at the end of your story, you might begin to doubt your ability to tell jokes. In the future it could make you hesitate to tell the same story or another story like it.

Let's imagine that you say "Good morning!" to a person you are just getting to know. That person smiles warmly and says "Hello!" The chances are, based on this exchange, you will want to speak to that person again. Yet, if you received a blank look and no response, then you might think twice before you would give a warm and friendly greeting again. No matter what we do, the consequences of our behavior tend to influence whether or not we repeat that same or similar behavior in the future. Sometimes the consequences of our behavior are obvious, such as when people laugh at our jokes or return a smile. But at other times, the consequences are less obvious or more complex. We are not always sure what kind of impact we are making on others until they tell us. It can be a blind area in our relationships.

FEEDBACK DEFINED

Interpersonal feedback is a term that has been borrowed from electronics. Information is fed back into a system so that corrections can be made. Thermostats, for example, use information about temperature to activate the air conditioning or heating units in our homes. Our outer space vehicles are equipped with guidance systems which feed information into navigation equipment and this information helps correct the rocket's course and keep it on line.

In a similar sense, information (consequences) in the form of feedback can be helpful to individuals to give them a better idea of how they are being received by others. With this information, they can either continue to do what they are doing (staying in the same track) or change their behavior (chart a new direction).

Suppose you found yourself in the following situation. A friend of yours has been appearing in the school play. After the opening night performance, your friend approached you and said, after some discussion of the play: "Now, come on, tell me. Be honest. How do you think that we did? Give me some feedback." Would it make any difference whether you had a positive or negative impression? Where would you begin?

Suppose that another student gave you an English paper to look over before turning it in for a grade. "Hey, give me some feedback on this paper, will you? What do you think?" If the paper was full of errors and was not outstanding, what would you do? Are you afraid that your honesty and candidness would endanger your friendship? How would you respond?

Feedback may be defined in many ways. For our purposes, it is not an opinion or judgment. It is not telling people whether they are right or wrong, or whether their work is good or bad. For the most part, feedback avoids making an evaluation.

Facilitative feedback is telling other persons the kind of impact that their behavior is having on you. Feedback involves an honest reaction of how a person affects you. When given properly, it offers people an opportunity to understand themselves better and to change, if they decide to do so.

THE FACILITATIVE FEEDBACK MODEL

Over the years we have learned some things about giving feedback. There are some things to avoid and there are some things to do. Here are some helpful guidelines:

WHAT TO DO

The facilitative feedback model has three simple parts:

1. **Be specific about the persons behavior.**
   (Be descriptive and give an example, if you can)
2. **Tell how the person's behavior makes you feel.**
3. **Tell what your feelings make you want to do.**

Let's examine the following examples. Can you identify the three parts?

"David, sometimes I come to school and I'm not feeling very well. I don't like being here. But when you greet me with your warm smile and you say something like: 'How's it going?', it makes me feel more relaxed and comfortable here. My 'blahs' go away and I usually try to get back to my work after we've talked a little."

See if you can identify the three parts in this example:

"You know, Joan, I wasn't sure the other day whether I should try out for the debate team. Then you began telling me that I make a good impression when I speak and I'm persuasive. I began thinking about what you said and it gave me the confidence to get a script and read over the play. Now I'm encouraged about trying out and I'm really looking forward to it. It also made me want to tell you how important our little conversation was the other day."

How about this one?

"As you know, Barbara, I have been wearing my hair long for a few years now and I really wasn't sure whether I should get it cut. I decided to plunge and you were one of the first ones to tell me that you liked the way it looked. I really appreciated that because I was a little regretful for a while. After your comments, I felt myself relax a lot more and then I began to enjoy my new hairstyle."

WHAT TO AVOID

Some of the things that you will want to avoid are:

(1) Giving advice.

(2) Judging or labeling.

(3) Focusing on things that can't be changed.

Look at this feedback:

"The trouble with you is that you're lazy. If you'd just sit down and study more, you wouldn't have trouble passing this class. You are never going to graduate if you don't get on the ball and quit acting like somebody owes you something. What you need to do is get yourself a study schedule and. . . ."

As you can see, in this example the person was bombarding the other with advice. The person was being judgmental and, no doubt, this kind of "feedback" was not very helpful. It likely was making the person feel guilty, anxious and defensive. It may even have provoked an argument, as most advice does.

Attaching a label to a person is not very helpful unless you can be more specific about what the person has done to make you reach that conclusion. *People don't like to be labeled.* They want to be seen as unique and not like everybody else. When you label individuals, you see them as just one of the pack and it may not be clear what it is they do that has earned them this label.

For example, witness this kind of feedback:

"One thing I noticed about you is that you are a nice person. In fact, you are one of the nicest persons in school. If others had a personality more like you, we would be much better off around here."

In examples like this one, persons may think that they are being complimentary and giving positive feedback. Actually, the feedback is not very effective because it relies on a label (nice person) and is not specific enough about the "nice behavior." Even though the positive statement: "You're a nice person," has a pleasant impact at first, the person might later begin to think: "I wonder what it is I do that makes them think that I'm so nice?"

Since we avoid giving advice, and we also avoid judging and labeling, it makes sense that we focus feedback on behaviors that could be changed.

VARYING THE FEEDBACK MODEL

Let's look at the three parts of the feedback model again:

Part 1—Be specific about the behavior.

"Yesterday we were talking about our problems with parents. Billy, you told me that you decided to sit down and work some things out, including privacy in your own bedroom."

Part 2—Tell how the person's behavior makes you feel.

"Well, it started me thinking. I got the courage to try the same thing with my parents."

Part 3—Tell what your feelings make you want to do.

"I wasn't sure how it was going to work out, but I did talk with my mother about it. She thinks we should have a family conference. I'm really glad you and I talked."

In this situation, the person giving the feedback begins by being specific about Billy's behavior. In some cases, however, it may be more convenient or easier to begin with your feelings and then tell what happened to give you those feelings. For instance:

"You know I was really uptight with you. I wasn't sure about talking with you. I wasn't sure how you felt about me. (Part 2) *But, after you sat with some of us at lunch the other day and began telling us about your interest in model airplanes, I began to see a different side of you. You laughed and seemed friendly.* (Part 1) *I just decided that I wanted to tell you that I've had some wrong impressions of you and I'd enjoy getting to know you better."* (Part 3)

Can you identify the three parts of the feedback model in the following example?

Part_____

"Some things have been happening here at school that made me want to come and talk with you."

Part_____

"You see, the other day there was some cheating going on in class. You suspected it and asked if anyone knew about it. You looked so angry that I just couldn't speak up at the time.

Part_____

"I was scared and afraid that if I did, matters would be worse. I thought it would be a lot easier to talk with you in private."

SOME HELPFUL GUIDELINES

Feedback can be a very powerful tool. It is especially pleasant to hear people tell us how we have made a positive impact on them. It creates a warm feeling and their statements can be very confirming. It is a great experience.

You can help others feel important by tuning in to some of the pleasant feelings you get when they do certain things. Tell them about it. With the exception of using the three parts of the model, there are no guidelines needed when you speak about your pleasant feelings—giving positive feedback. Just try it! You'll like it!

On the other hand, we have learned that when we share some of our unpleasant feelings, there are three guidelines that may be helpful. These are:

1. Do you have some "chips in the bank?"

This is another way of saying: "Have you taken the time to listen to the person? Have you tried to be understanding?" Every time you are a good listener and use high facilitative responses (Chapter 3), you are building up some "chips in the bank"— you are building a reserve that can be drawn upon at a later time. In fact, some people have said that after listening and trying to understand the person better, their unpleasant feelings disappeared. Thus, it was not necessary to give negative feedback.

If you have someone in mind who strikes you in an unpleasant way, make a concentrated effort to listen to them and to increase the frequency of the high facilitative responses—no matter the topic. You will probably gain a better idea of whether or not you want to speak up regarding your unpleasant feelings.

There are times, of course, when you will not be able to build up that reserve in advance. For example, you might have just met someone. You will have to gamble that some negative feedback (speaking about your unpleasant feelings) will not bankrupt the relationship. However, even a few "chips in the bank" previous to your feedback may be helpful.

2. Is your unpleasant feeling a persistent one?

Nobody likes a grouch. Therefore, it is not wise to "pop off" at everything and everybody that causes you some unpleasantness. Have some tolerance.

Our life is full of daily conflicts and you will probably not respond to everyone who upsets you. However, it is unwise to let matters build up to the point of "boiling over." Then you have a "mess" to clean up and the feedback model is not as effective. When persistent feelings are left to simmer and boil, then the relationship suffers. Therefore, you will want to speak up about your feelings, but let them be persistent and timely.

3. What words will best communicate your ideas?

The third helpful guidelines emphasizes that you should be careful in the selection of your words. If you are too intense and choose words that are loaded with a lot of emotion, you run the risk of not being heard at all. The person may become so defensive that the impact of your feedback is diminished.

There are many shades of meanings. Let your inner experience help you to find the most appropriate feeling word. For example, it is not helpful to tell other people that you "hate" them, when, in fact, what they do "irritates" or "annoys" you. Likewise, the term "love" can, at times, be too powerful or too intense for some persons. You might prefer to use a word like "close," "care," "warm," "affectionate" or whatever. Obviously, the choice of words depends upon the situation and your own judgment.

THE VALUE OF FEEDBACK

Feedback releases tension. Although it may be difficult to say (or receive) at the moment, if it is important enough, you will take the time to use the model. The model is systematic. It offers you some degree of control over your own emotions. It not only generates, but releases energy. After you have given feedback to someone, regardless of whether it was positive or negative, it's not a time to say: "Whew, I'm glad that's over." Rather, it's a time to really focus on the other person and tune in. It's a time once again to be a good listener and to make high facilitative responses.

Giving and receiving feedback can be threatening or thrilling. Feedback effectiveness depends on timing and readiness. Obviously, the more chips you have built up in the bank, the more likely the person will be receptive to hearing what you have to say. If you are working with an individual who is extremely defensive—who has built up a shell—then your words will bounce off, much like water off a turtle's back. On the other hand, if you can encourage that person to talk with you in a personal conversation, one that is full of honesty and respect, then feedback will be helpful.

When the feedback model is used, it makes the relationship closer, no matter whether the focus is on pleasant or unpleasant feelings. Without feedback, a relationship is incomplete. There would be too many blind areas. With feedback, a relationship can grow. Communication will be more open. There is an increased self-awareness and an added dimension of being responsible for what one does.

While change is sometimes implied, persons who receive feedback are always responsible for whether or not they want to continue or to change their behavior. If you don't know how your behavior affects others or what impact you are having on them, then how can you ever change?

Here are some more hints when giving feedback:

Be concise— Too many times people get wordy and the feedback message is lost.

Be authentic—The feedback model can be powerful, but when a person is phony and attempts to disguise real feelings, it falls flat.

Be appropriate— The timing of feedback is important. If you rush in with feedback before you've had a chance to build some trust and understanding, it could be seen as either premature or inappropriate.

Be involved—Feedback should not be used lightly. Don't give someone feedback unless you are willing to be responsible for what you say. You should also be willing to let the person engage you in a conversation that might clarify matters.

FEEDBACK AS PRAISE

Praise has been termed a *social reinforcer.* We like to hear people say nice things about us. If praise is given honestly, it provides us with a warm feeling, a flush of excitement and some self-pride. Sometimes, however, praise can be so lavish or so unexpected that it causes embarrassment and perhaps some shyness.

Most people in our society are not used to receiving compliments. To the contrary, our society appears to be based on criticism. We often find that teachers and parents have a tendency to criticize more than praise. Criticism is a part of the "old Puritan work ethic" that has haunted us for years: "We can always do better." No matter how well we think we have done a job, there always seems to be something that we could have done more.

For example, when you turn in a paper to an English class, most teachers have a tendency to mark those things that were wrong, thus drawing attention to the negative aspects.

Praise can be helpful. Some educators have even admonished teachers to "catch a child being good" and then reinforce that child with praise. Praise is supposed to build self-confidence, increase security, motivate more learning, generate good will and improve human relations. If it can do all that, then why don't we hear more praise?

Praise is not a panacea. It is a positive evaluation of a person or an act. If it comes across as insincere flattery, then it will have little or no impact. Interestingly enough, some statements of praise, even when they are sincere, can produce the opposite results. For instance, suppose that the following statements were made to you: "You are such a great student. You're probably the best in the class." At first glance it may seem like these statements would make you feel more confident and that you are appreciated. On second thought, however, you might find yourself becoming a little more defensive. "Ah, you are just saying that to make me feel good!" or "Really? Well, I do try, but I'm not always sure how it will turn out."

Sometimes statements of praise create discomfort and make us feel less confident. It's not easy to handle praise, especially when it focuses on labeling our personality: "You are such a good person." "You are always so thoughtful and sensitive." "You are always pleasant to be around and never say an unkind word." This kind of praise can make us feel uneasy, even though at first it might be viewed as pleasant.

Haim Ginott, a famous child psychologist, has given us some helpful hints regarding praise: *"Praise that evaluates personality and character is unpleasant, unsafe. Praise that describes efforts, accomplishments and feelings is helpful and safe."* He goes on to suggest: *"Describe, don't evaluate. Deal with events, don't appraise personality. Describe feelings, don't evaluate character. Give a realistic picture of the accomplishment, don't glorify the person."*

When we describe behaviors or events and our specific feelings related to these behaviors or events, it allows the people receiving the feedback to draw their own conclusions about their personality, character and behavior. As a result of expressing our pleasant feelings and being specific about the behavior, a person may conclude: *"I am liked, I am respected, I am appreciated, I am capable, I am valued."*

FEEDBACK AS CONFRONTATION

There are, of course, times when you feel a confrontation is necessary. The term "confrontation" has many meanings. To some people it means judging, lecturing or acting in some punitive way. As suggested earlier, this kind of behavior is rarely effective, even if your intent is to be helpful.

Sometimes the term "confrontation" has been used when describing a statement that points to a contradiction, a misinterpretation, an inconsistency or some kind of discrepancy in a person's talk. But even this kind of confrontation has questionable value. Unless presented through the feedback model, it runs the danger of falling into the trap of being judgmental, critical and from a superior and authoritarian position.

A dictionary definition of confrontation indicates a facing of another, especially a challenge. While a confrontation may be challenging, it need not be destructive. Whether or not a confrontation is effective will probably depend upon the words that are used and the intent. Confronting is a risk and it takes a commitment. You must *care* about the other person.

Confrontations can range from a light challenge to a strong statement. Sometimes it can precipitate a conflict—at least a temporary one. The balance of the relationship may be temporarily disrupted. However, this need not be a crisis that goes unresolved. Confrontation is not just a challenge, an opinion, a threat or a deliberate exposure. *Confrontation is a form of feedback, whereby people learn about something they have done that has created an unpleasant experience for us.*

In a confrontation anxiety increases. As anxiety increases, there is some resistance, some defensiveness and the relationship becomes a little closed. However, if the person has experienced you as a helping and caring person, then a confrontation need not be frightening or harmful to the relationship. It can be stimulating, challenging and help people come into more direct contact with themselves. It gives people more information about themselves, reducing some ambiguities and some blindspots.

You may want to stop now and use the activities at the end of this chapter to help you get a better understanding of the feedback model and its parts. Experience the process. Then, read on to see another way of giving feedback.

DIRECT AND INDIRECT FEEDBACK

The facilitative feedback model described previously might be viewed as *direct feedback.* In this case you are speaking directly about the person's behavior and your feelings. You are telling the person what those feelings make you want to do. This approach is the most straight forward.

Another form of giving feedback might be called *indirect feedback.* In this situation, metaphors or descriptions are used to describe the impact that a person is having on us.

Indirect feedback uses objects, animals or fantasized ideas which help communicate our experiences to other persons. Sometimes a picture is worth a thousand words. The more descriptive we can be of that picture, the more it will communicate our thoughts and feelings. Indirect feedback has a lighter tone than direct feedback. It sometimes allows us to say some confronting things that would otherwise be too uncomfortable in the direct feedback model.

Let's look at some examples of indirect feedback:

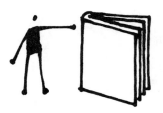

Example 1:

"Joanne, you remind me of a book. This is a book with a very pretty cover and one that captures my attention. I can't walk by without wanting to know more about the book. When I open the cover I see a lot of words and I see how complex the book is—how much there really is to it. At first I wasn't sure that I wanted to know that much. But, as I read the first few chapters, I learned that you're full of mystery, excitement, fun and you have a lot of interesting ideas. The book isn't as difficult to read as I thought it might be. Now, I look forward to reading some of the next chapters."

Example 2:

"Hey, Dad, I see you as a big old oak tree standing out in an open pasture. It's the kind of tree that provides lots of shade and comfort, especially when it gets really hot. I can sense its strength and know that it is going to be there. Sometimes when things get really tough, I just want to sit under the tree and enjoy the shade that it provides and the security that I feel."

Example 3:

"Andrea, you remind me of a sponge. This is one of those beautiful decorative sponges with many different colors. It's a marvelous sponge. It's the kind I don't mind having around. It soaks up everything that takes place. Sometimes I wonder, however, what's in the sponge now that it has soaked up all of the ideas? But, the sponge never says anything and sometimes I get curious and want to reach over and squeeze this sponge to find out what it is holding back."

Example 4:

"Ralph, I see you as a race car. A car with racing stripes down its side and painted in bright colors. Everyone admires the car and stands around wondering about it. It seems to have so much appeal, but it simply just sits. After a while I'm just like some of the rest and I begin to wonder if it will ever race. Some of the people walk away. I've started to think that maybe that is what I should do too, but I can't help thinking that if it had the right fuel it would really take off and win a lot of races."

Example 5:

"You remind me of a cat, Mary Ann. A cat that is resting in front of a warm fireplace in a mountain lodge. It's a furry cat and one that enjoys being petted on certain occasions. At other times the cat will run away and, if cornered, will strike back. I'm thinking of the cat now and wishing that I could move closer, but I'm very aware that the cat has sharp claws and could hurt me. So, with mixed feelings, I admire the cat but have decided to walk on by. I don't think this is the time to be close."

Example 6:

"When I think of you, I see a typewriter. It is a magic typewriter that can type faster than any other machine ever invented. It's decorated in many colors and as it types it also plays music. I respect your ability to write and use words. I really envy the way you can talk and give speeches in class. However, the speed of the typewriter gets going so fast, sometimes, that I want to reach over and slow it down so I can understand the words and appreciate the music."

Do you get a picture of the people? In all of these examples, the speaker was attempting to be descriptive about an object. A metaphor can be helpful only if it is complete with such things as location, size, color, feel and so forth. Of course, it is necessary that you tell how it makes you feel to be around or with the object. You can see in each of the examples that the people probably learned something about themselves. Try to make up some of your own examples.

1. Think of a person in your class. Think of that person now as an object and describe the object here:

2. List here some feeling words that you get when you are with or around the object (person):

3. Write here some things that you would like to do with the object or that you feel like doing when you are around the object:

USING FEEDBACK IN A GROUP

When feedback is used in a group situation, the facilitator can help the members follow the facilitative model. For instance, when a person gives a label (e.g. You are a smart person), then that person could be assisted to be more specific about any behavior that led to that label or conclusion.

A facilitator might say: "What did (name) do that made you reach that conclusion?" This then might be followed by asking the person what feelings are experienced.

Suppose someone has said in a group: "This is a boring group and I wish I weren't here." This person might be encouraged to tell what happened in the group to bring about some of the boredom.

It should be remembered that we speak for ourselves and not for the group. When giving feedback in a group, there is no need for consensus or agreement on feedback. Even if more than one person uses the same metaphor, as in indirect feedback, it takes on new and personal meaning with each speaker.

Let's look at some examples of giving feedback to a group:

Leader of group one:

"Today I was a little late getting here. When I arrived, I saw that all of you had gotten here before me and were working on the project we discussed last week. Frankly, I was really relieved to know that everything was going well and it made me want to say that I am proud of you as a group." (Direct Feedback)

Leader of group two:

"You know, this group reminds me of a herd of horses. I look out over the pasture and I can see some of the horses just standing there and enjoying the sunshine, munching away on the grass, relaxing and having a good time. Some others are running around, scrambling, kicking up dust and making it generally uncomfortable for others. I'm proud of the herd, but I'm not always sure exactly what I should do about some of the disturbances. Perhaps it doesn't bother those of you who are relaxing and doing your work. Can we talk about it? What do you think?" (Indirect Feedback)

Many people have used the facilitative feedback model (direct and indirect forms). Those who have learned to integrate it into their everyday relationships report that it has been helpful in communicating their thoughts and feelings about others. It slows them down—enough for them to get some control. It has a calming influence that enables them to choose words carefully. After all, they want to communicate effectively.

Using the model is no different than using good paragraphs to write a theme in English or using a mathematical formula to solve a problem in physics. A step-by-step approach can be systematic, but it is not meant to be restrictive.

Like other things that you have experienced about interpersonal skills, the facilitative feedback model may seem a little awkward at first. Continue to practice it. As you become more skilled in its use, you will find that you have a very valuable tool for both your individual and group work.

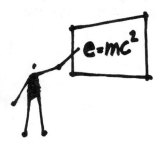

Activity 5.1:
POSITIVE FEEDBACK (GO-AROUND)

PURPOSE:

To practice giving and receiving positive feedback and to help you learn more about yourself.

MATERIALS:

None.

PROCEDURE:

(1) Form a small group, about five people to a group. Get with people that you would like to talk with, telling them the impact they have on you and learning about the impact that you have on them.

(2) Review in your own mind, or perhaps in discussion with others, the three parts (steps) of giving feedback.

(3) Someone in the circle should volunteer to begin. The first volunteer then talks to each person in the group, in turn, giving each some positive feedback. The person receiving the feedback listens and makes no comments. *After the first volunteer has given each person in the group some feedback, another person then volunteers and gives feedback to each person.* Again, each member listens to the feedback and makes no comments. It can be helpful if you: a) call the person by name, b) look at them and c) talk directly to them.

(4) After the last person in the group has practiced giving feedback, have a group discussion about the experience. You may want to ask some questions or get some clarification about what was said.

THE ABSENT PERSON

PURPOSE:

To practice using the feedback model outlined in this chapter by focusing on someone outside the class.

MATERIALS:

An empty chair.

PROCEDURE:

(1) Form a circle with about five to six people. An empty chair is placed in the middle.

(2) Think of someone who is *not* sitting in the circle. As you think of that person, what is something that they do that you like? What kind of a pleasant feeling do you get? Then, when you have that feeling, what do you want to do?

(3) Now, imagine that the person is sitting in the empty chair. Tell that person your thoughts, using the feedback model outlined in this chapter.

(4) After everyone has had a turn focusing on the positive, think of a person with whom you have had an *unpleasant* experience. Using the model and imagining that they are in the chair, give that person some feedback.

(5) Discuss the experience after everyone has had a turn.

Activity 5.3:
USING FEEDBACK WITH OTHERS

PURPOSE:

To practice giving feedback.

MATERIALS:

Paper; pencil/pen.

PROCEDURE:

(1) Review the steps of the feedback model to yourself. During a conversation with someone outside the class, use the feedback model. It may be with someone who is close to you or with someone you know only casually.

Spontaneously work the feedback response into the conversation. Make a mental note of the wording you used and the person's reactions or comments.

(2) Write a description of the experience, reporting your words and the words of the other person as closely as you can. Tell what the outcome, if any, seemed to be.

(3) Share your paper with someone else in the class who also tried the assignment.

Chapter VI

Not to decide is to decide.

responsible decision-making

We are confronted every day with different situations that require us to make a decision. Some are more serious than others. Consider the following:

It's late on a Friday afternoon and Wade's family has just sat down to eat their evening meal. His parents announce that tomorrow the entire family is going to visit Aunt Joan and Uncle Phillip who live 150 miles away. Wade would like to see them, but he has already made plans to go to the lake—with a group of his friends. . . .

Jessica's final year in high school has rolled around and the pressure of being accepted into a college is increasing. Her parents favor the state's largest institution and their alma mater. Most of her friends are going to the college sixty miles away. Jessica's first choice is a small out-of-state school, which seems to be more of what she really wants. . . .

After seventeen years of marriage, Walt's parents decided that they no longer want to live together. Each parent wants Walt to live with them. He loves and cares deeply for both parents and doesn't want to hurt either one's feelings. He realizes that he must make his decision. . . soon!

Angie has had it with her parents. It seems like all they ever do is argue, either with each other or with Angie. Once again, Angie has been put on restriction and is stuck at home for the next two weeks. One of her friends, who is also unhappy with her parents, is going to take off and leave home. She asks Angie if she wants to go.

Sabrina's girlfriends have been experimenting with drugs. It's something new to all of them. They are encouraging her to join them at Gloria's house after school to "get high." Sabrina has mixed feelings. She feels that she could get caught and this would disappoint her parents and boyfriend, who disapprove of using drugs for excitement. On the other hand, she wants to be liked by her friends and fears that they will exclude her from other get-to-gethers in the future if she does not attend. As the end of the school day nears, Sabrina opens a note that says: "We are meeting at the water fountain before we go to Gloria's. Don't be late!"

There is no way to escape decision-making. From the time we are born until the time we die, life continually bombards us with a dazzling array of possibilities from which to choose. While many decisions are relatively easy to make, some are quite demanding of time and energy. Moreover, some decisions, more than others, seem to have the potential for making a profound influence on the direction and quality of our lives.

George Orwell, in his science fiction classic, *1984*, described vividly a society which offered its citizenry few opportunities to make decisions. People were told where to live, what job to hold, what materials to read and even what thoughts and ideas to think. The all-powerful government assumed total responsibility for deciding the quality of life for each person. In the end, the people became passive participants in their own lives, obeying that which the government decided was best for them. They surrendered their own potential for determining the paths their lives would follow. Personal responsibility for one's destiny did not exist.

In the book, *Future Shock*, Alvin Toffler described some events that are taking place in contemporary society. Contrary to that which Orwell had predicted, Toffler wrote of the present as offering *more and more alternatives from which to choose*. He outlined the effects that resulted from the amazing technological advances of the past fifty to sixty years. In discussing what he has termed the "death of permanance," Toffler says that much of the conflict and confusion which exists within people today is, to a great extent, the result of having to continually make choices from all the alternatives that are now available. Many people are finding it harder and harder to decide what is worth caring about—what is worth their time and energy.

We are forced to choose from among alternatives that didn't even exist some years ago. For example, many young people in junior and senior high schools are exposed to a number of illicit drugs, especially marijuana. While use of these drugs was not an option in many schools in the past, today most young people must make a conscious choice and take a stand as to whether or not they want to experiment with drugs. If their answer is "yes," even that decision brings more alternatives and more decisions:"What drug or drugs am I willing to try? How often? Under what circumstances? What are the consequences?"

We all want to make decisions that will result in a more positive and enhancing lifestyle. We want to choose wisely. Yet, often times we are confused and uncertain as to *how to decide*. Ideally, it is to our advantage when we have the time to think through situations and examine all of the alternatives. Even then, however, we cannot be sure that we are going to make the best decision. On too many occasions, we find ourselves in situations when time forces us to make quick decisions. Of course, the more aware we are of ourselves as people—what we value and what we believe in—the better we are able to make decisions and live by them.

Decision-making is a skill that can be practiced and improved upon. You can learn to make more self-enhancing, personally-rewarding decisions—decisions that you are pleased with and which will stand the test of time. It is a skill that can promote personal happiness and give you a sense of being in control of your life.

Almost anyone who has thought about good decision-making has suggested that you begin by identifying the problem, followed by generating alternatives and gathering information. Finally, you make a decision and try it out. A case might be built for the following statement: "We are always making decisions. From the time we get up in the morning until we go to bed at night, we are faced with decisions. Life is a continuous decision-making process."

No matter what we do, we have to live with it. Unfortunately, many people tend to live their lives haphazardly and spend little time approaching life in a thoughtful way.

A FIVE-STEP DECISION-MAKING PROCESS

Not all situations lend themselves to the luxury of a carefully thought out plan. But, a five-step process can serve as a guide— a plan of action—that can be helpful in decision-making. Let's look at these five steps:

1. **Identify the central issue or problem.**
2. **Explore the issue or problem: alternatives and consequences.**
3. **Choose a next step.**
4. **Act upon your choice.**
5. **Evaluate the results.**

STEP 1: IDENTIFY THE CENTRAL ISSUE OR PROBLEM.

An important first step is to identify all the important aspects of the problem or situation. For example, it might be helpful to answer these kinds of questions:

What is the problem?

When does it occur and under what circumstances?

Who else is involved or who else contributes to the problem?

Who or what interferes with making a decision?

Sometimes the pressure of deciding can be so overwhelming that it prevents us from taking any action at all. If we first sort out and clearly identify the issues or the problem, then other steps in the decision-making process make more sense. Unfortunately, sometimes a problem can be complicated. If we cannot define the problem, then we compound our difficulties, sometimes thinking and acting on issues that are really not of any significance.

One important key to identifying the problem is to think of it in specific terms. For example, what is Sabrina's problem? She can not avoid making a decision, one way or another. What should Sabrina do? Will she do what her friends want her to do or will she follow the wishes of her parents and boyfriend? Or, will she make a decision based on an understanding of her own values and, regardless of the decision, be willing to accept responsibility for it?

One helpful approach is to list on a piece of paper the issues that are involved. Try to state the problem as precisely as you can. Examine the words that you use. Circle the most important words or terms. Why these words? What special meaning do they have?

Unfortunately, the "eye can not see the eyeball." Thinking to yourself about all of the related issues can be confusing. The more you think, the more frustrated you become. The more frustrating, the more confusion and anxiety. Sometimes, when we are in this state, we become indecisive and let others make decisions for us.

Still another approach is to talk with someone—someone who is an attentive listener and who will help you to clarify the issues involved. This person can be especially helpful if your ability to make decisions is respected. That person's role is that of a clarifier—to ask searching questions. Of course, this is one of the main reasons why many people are interested in the work of peer facilitators. More and more, people are seeing the advantage of being open about their problems and the decisions they are trying to make.

STEP 2: EXPLORE THE ISSUE OR PROBLEM: ALTERNATIVES AND CONSEQUENCES.

Every situation involves a weighing and balancing of the many forces that are part of the problem. As we attempt to explore a situation, it is necessary to look at the alternatives and the consequences of any decision. To *not* make a decision, of course, is to make a decision. The alternatives and consequences of being indecisive can also be examined. It is important to be as clear as possible regarding our values and attitudes in relation to alternatives and consequences.

Examine the alternatives

Almost every situation presents a number of options. We might view some of the possible alternatives as undesirable. Nevertheless, there are alternatives. Thus, a conscious choice can be made. Sometimes we say: "I have no choice. . . ." However, with very rare exceptions (e.g. being born, aging, natural disasters and death), *we do have a choice.*

Remember Jessica? She was faced with the dilemma of choosing a college. Torn between pleasing her parents and doing what her friends were doing, she also wanted to do what she felt was right for her. In this situation, Jessica might think: "I just have to go to my parents' alma mater. They would be disappointed if I didn't. Besides, they are paying my way. I guess there is nothing else that I can do."

In helping Jessica make a decision, one important step is to help her recognize that she can choose to go to her parents' alma mater and please her parents, but she doesn't have to go there. There are other options available for her, even though some of them may create some temporary anxiety and some problems for others. If Jessica consciously considers all her alternatives, her final decision has more significance and she will probably have fewer regrets later. Thus, after the problem has been identified, it is important to ask: "What are all the possible alternatives?"

Determine the probable consequences.

Have you ever heard someone say: "If I had known that it was going to work out this way, I would never have done it." Every alternative has its consequences. Considering the probable results of a particular alternative can lead to more intelligent and positive decisions.

Wade had to choose between visiting his aunt and uncle or going to a lake with his close friends. His dilemma might be resolved by his thoughtful consideration of the consequences. He will want to think about how his aunt and uncle would feel and how his parents would respond if he says he doesn't want to go. How will his friends react if he tells them that he has changed his mind? He will also want to think about how he will respond to these reactions.

While Wade can never know with 100 percent accuracy what the consequences of his choice will be, it is possible for him to estimate the *probable consequences*. Therefore, the second question to be answered is: "What are the probable consequences of my choosing any of the alternatives?"

Relate alternatives and consequences to values.

Perhaps the "bottom line" in any decision has to do with our own value system. After exploring alternatives and consequences, we do what seems to be the best for us. The final decision must reflect what we believe to be most important. It is something that we must be willing to live with.

While we are aware of many of our attitudes, feelings and beliefs, we frequently are unsure of what we value—what it is that is so dear to us. Our personal value system is the core of who we are and what we stand for. Clarifying what it is that we value is an integral part of making a thoughtful and personally enhancing decision. We choose our pathway by the light of our values.

STEP 3: CHOOSE A NEXT STEP.

After having looked at alternatives and consequences, and after having weighed these against our value system, it is time to make a decision—to choose. Regardless of the way in which our decision turns out, it is something that we have considered and do not have to apologize for. If this decision proves to be one that is not as satisfying as we had anticipated, then we examine the factors that led to our decision and try to make a new decision, one that will improve the situation. *If we are systematic in making our first decision, we will probably spend less time regretting our choice.*

We each have the power and capacity to make decisions that are the most advantageous to us and for others who are directly affected by our choice. We can make decisions that give thought, not only to our own interests, but to the interests of others. After all, we do not live in isolation. We realize that, more often than not, others are affected by our decisions. Yet, others should not be responsible for our decisions and they should not make decisions for us. It is our choice and we must choose the next step.

STEP 4: ACT UPON YOUR CHOICE.

Once we have made our decision and decided upon a next step, it is time to put that choice into action. Acting upon our decisions can sometimes make us anxious. We now realize that we are going to experience the results of our deciding and there is no more time for hypothesizing and fantasizing. The moment of truth has arrived.

For instance, even though Walt wanted to have his parents live together so that they could continue to be a family, certain decisions had been made which affected Walt. He, in turn, had to make a decison. If he had been part of the decision-making process regarding the divorce, there is no doubt that he would have recommended the alternative of remaining together as a family. Now, it is his turn to make a decision. He can not live with both parents. No matter who he chooses to live with, there is going to be some sadness and disappointment.

Even after the decision is made, there may be some second guessing, some doubtfulness and Walt may wonder whether or not he made the right choice. No doubt Walt would like to look into the future to reassure himself that his choice is the right one. But, since he does not have this alternative (looking into a crystal ball), he must be willing to cope with some of the unpleasant aspects that will inevitably result in his decision.

Making decisions can be a time in our lives when we prove to ourselves and others that we are responsible—that we can determine what happens to us. *Systematic decision-making is a process of self-management.* It enables us to feel better about the direction in which we are moving. *We are what we do.* By acting upon our decisions, we dramatically illustrate that *our deeds in life are a reflection of our creeds about life.*

Step 5: EVALUATE THE RESULTS.

The final step involves our evaluating and analyzing the outcomes of what we have done. In the first few steps, we can only hypothesize and estimate the probable outcomes. At this point, we have acted upon one of the alternatives and have experienced its consequences. We now need to ask the question: "How am I feeling about what has happened as a result of my decision?"

Our personal values system will be of help in evaluating the results. We may begin the process of making decisions again. Based on results from other decisions, new alternatives may be chosen and new directions sought. Or, we may be proud of our wisdom for having chosen wisely and positively, and celebrate the results.

This is the time for feedback, a time to learn more about ourselves and our environment. The more intimately we experience ourselves and our surroundings, the easier it becomes to predict the results that may come from our decisions. Our awareness of relationships and our environment can be heightened by taking time to reflect on the consequences which result from the choices we make. Most important, this tends to increase the probability of making wiser choices in the future.

There is no way to escape making decisions. By not deciding to be an active participant in your life, you are in effect choosing to let other people determine your existence. Thus, you choose to be passive, to ride with the tide.

The more effective, rational and self-enhancing path is to be a decision-maker, to set your own direction, to take more responsibility for your own life. The more you use the decision-making process, the more skilled you will become.

Activity 6.1:
SETTING PRIORITIES

PURPOSE:

To practice the skill of decision-making by becoming more aware of alternatives and values.

MATERIALS:

None.

PROCEDURE:

Look at each of the following rank ordered questions. Write a No. 1 to indicate your top priority, a No. 2 for your second priority and a No. 3 for your lowest priority:

A. What is the most important characteristic that your boy/girl friend can possess?

_____ good-looking

_____ fun at parties

_____ intelligent

B. Where would you rather be on a Saturday afternoon?

_____ watching a sports program on T.V.

_____ at the beach

_____ on a picnic with your family

C. What is the one thing about school that you would really like to see changed?

_____ the grading system

_____ going five days a week

_____ the teachers

D. Which would you "least" like to be?

_____ very poor

_____ confined to a wheelchair

_____ blind

E. Which would you give up, if you had to?

_____ religious freedom

_____ economic freedom

_____ political freedom

Activity 6.2:
GOOD DECISIONS—POOR DECISIONS

PURPOSE:

To explore the process of decision-making; to become more aware that all decisions have consequences.

MATERIALS:

Notes About Me notebook, pencil/pen.

PROCEDURE:

(1) Divide one page of your notebook in half. Mark the top half of the page "Good Decisions." Mark the words "Poor Decisions" on the bottom section.

(2) Thinking back over some important decisions you have made during the past six months, categorize them according to results. Write key words describing the decision in the appropriate section.

(3) Look at the "Good Decisions" section. Ask yourself the following questions:

    A. How did I come to make these decisions?

    B. Who was influential in my making the decision?

    C. How many of these decisions were the result of my having received advice from others?

(4) Ask these same questions as you look at the "Poor Decisions" section.

(5) Now, write down your impressions of this activity. What did you learn or relearn?

Activity 6:3:

WESTERN UNION

PURPOSE:

To take a stand and act upon something that is important to you.

MATERIALS:

A three-inch by five-inch index card or a Western Union telegraph form, pencil/pen.

PROCEDURE:

(1) Design a Western Union form using the model below:

WESTERN UNION

Dear _____

Date _____

I urge you to _____

_____

_____

_____

Signed _____

(2) Complete the form using a real-life situation which you feel is important.

(3) Read the telegram in class and/or send it to the person involved.

Chapter VII

The important thing is this: to be able at any moment to sacrifice what we are for what we could become.

assessing self and others

Evaluation plays an important part in our lives. When used properly, evaluation procedures can provide us with the kind of information that we need in order to assess our progress, to make adjustments when necessary, to give us direction and to eventually help us understand more about our work.

People who resist evaluation or assessment usually claim that they are too busy or do not see any importance in it. Sometimes it's not even planned as part of their work. In other instances, some people feel that evaluation is not necessary because they have faith in what they are doing and sincerely believe that their work is helpful. They rely more on their intuition to help them assess themselves and their efforts. They count on testimonials—a few people who express their appreciation. While this can be one approach to learning more about ourselves and our work, it is not very systematic. Testimonials, therefore, provide a limited method of evaluation.

This chapter will focus on three important aspects of evaluation or assessment: first, *assessment of yourself as a helper*: second, *assessment of the helping process and skills used in your work*; and thirdly, *assessment of outcomes that you are trying to reach as a peer facilitator.*

ASSESSING THE SELF-CONCEPT

Who are you? What are your values? What do you believe? What are your goals? How do you think that most people would describe you? What things irritate you about others?

If you are going to be a helping person and if you want to facilitate others, then it is important to know something about yourself. After all, when you are working with another person, your personality is involved in the helping process. What you believe to be true will affect the way you relate with others. For instance, suppose you are a deeply religious person and believe that a lot of people could be helped, if only they would practice more of what your religion teaches you. Your religion is something special to you. You value it, you believe in it and try to follow it. Are those who take a different religious position so opposite from you that you are unable to work with them? Is there room in life for more than one way to worship? What part do your religious values play in working with others?

Suppose you have decided that you want to go to college. You want to learn more. You are convinced that a college education— regardless of career choice—is valuable by itself because it will help you learn more about the world and others. Does this mean that you will only be able to work with others who are planning to go to college? Should you only work with those who have similar educational interests? Are your values so different from those not going to college that you cannot communicate with them?

With preparation and practice, you are going to be able to work with and help a lot of different people regardless of age, sex, racial or social differences. But, you will need to know your own biases and prejudices. You will need to know what it is that you value most. It is important to be aware of those things that threaten you and make you defensive. If you cannot remain open in your relationships with others, then you run the risk of being minimally effective or not helpful at all. One step, then, in being a good helper is to engage in some self-assessment procedures. What do you bring to the helping relationship?

There are many methods that can be used to assess or evaluate yourself. These include: taking a personality inventory; completing a values checklist; writing a personal essay; listing some of your strengths and weaknesses; and asking others how they see you.

Because your self-concept can influence much of your behavior, it is important to know more about it. Self-concepts are highly personal matters and are often difficult to verbalize. However, attempts at describing yourself can bring about some insights regarding the things you do and the decisions you make. It is important to remember that our self-concepts do change from time to time. There are, of course, some characteristics about self that appear to be more stable than others and seem to have a predominate role in life.

What follows is a self-appraisal inventory. Find a private place and complete the inventory. Mark it as you see yourself now. Sometimes it can be helpful to put down the first response that comes to your mind. Be as candid and honest with yourself as you can. Being candid and honest is an important first step.

Table III

SELF-APPRAISAL INVENTORY

INSTRUCTIONS:

For each of the statements below, check the place on the scale which best describes your appraisal of the matter. (SA=Strongly Agree, A=Agree, NS=Not Sure, D=Disagree, SD=Strongly Disagree)

1. I have the ability to listen to others.   SA A NS D SD
2. I feel comfortable sharing my feelings with others.   SA A NS D SD
3. I have some understanding of why I do the things I do.   SA A NS D SD
4. I am tolerant of others.   SA A NS D SD
5. I am curious about what others think and feel.   SA A NS D SD
6. It is easy for me to be accepting of others' behaviors.   SA A NS D SD
7. I trust most people.   SA A NS D SD
8. I have an ability to influence others.   SA A NS D SD
9. I get along well with my peers.   SA A NS D SD
10. I have a clear idea of my goals in life.   SA A NS D SD
11. I know what I value and believe to be true.   SA A NS D SD
12. I work well alone and independent of others when I need to.   SA A NS D SD
13. I can keep a secret.   SA A NS D SD
14. I am able to assume responsibilities and follow things through.   SA A NS D SD
15. I enjoy solving problems.   SA A NS D SD
16. I can accept criticism from others.   SA A NS D SD
17. I care about my appearance.   SA A NS D SD
18. I am curious about what others think of me.   SA A NS D SD
19. I am a leader.   SA A NS D SD
20. I am optimistic about my future.   SA A NS D SD
21. I relate well with adults.   SA A NS D SD
22. I am happy with my body.   SA A NS D SD
23. Physical fitness is important to me.   SA A NS D SD

ASSESSING THE HELPING PROCESS

Enough research is now available to indicate that certain facilitative skills are valuable in the helping process. When we use these skills, it is more likely that we will be helpful. Therefore, it is important to assess whether or not these skills or behaviors are present in our work and whether or not they are creating a positive relationship that can bring about some desired outcomes.

Some peer facilitators view the opportunity to evaluate their work with mixed feelings. They want to do a good job; in fact, many want to be perfect if they can. Because they are working with people and feel some responsibility for the outcomes of their work, they want to perform faultlessly. For some, the idea that their work could be improved upon suggests to them that they didn't do a good job or that they were unqualified. This may not be the case. Rather, assessment and evaluation of the helping process simply means that we want to be *more responsible* for our work and use our work to become *even more effective* in the future.

We may become so involved in our work that it becomes difficult to be objective. Sometimes other people can help us evaluate our efforts because they are not as personally involved. However, it is important to recognize that we will not always have objective help. We must learn to identify our own skills and to assess our own performances.

What follows is a *Facilitative Skills Checklist.* It focuses on your behaviors as a facilitator. After you have completed the checklist, you might want to sit down with another peer and share your results. Perhaps through discussion you can clarify some matters. Maybe you will want to talk with the peer trainer about some of the items.

Table IV
FACILITATIVE SKILLS CHECKLIST

INSTRUCTIONS:

Think of your peer facilitator experiences. Indicate the extent of your agreement with each of the following statements by marking the scale: (SA=Strongly Agree, A=Agree, NS=Not Sure, D=Disagree, SD=Strongly Disagree).

1. I maintain good eye contact.	SA A NS D SD
2. Most of my verbal comments follow the lead of the other person.	SA A NS D SD
3. I encourage others to talk about feelings.	SA A NS D SD
4. I am able to ask open-ended questions.	SA A NS D SD
5. I can restate or clarify a person's ideas.	SA A NS D SD
6. I can respond to the basic ideas of a long statement made by a person.	SA A NS D SD
7. I can make statements that reflect the person's feelings.	SA A NS D SD
8. I can share my feelings relevant to the discussion.	SA A NS D SD
9. I am able to give feedback to my helpee.	SA A NS D SD
10. At least 75% or more of my responses are high facilitative.	SA A NS D SD
11. I can assist the person to list some alternatives available.	SA A NS D SD
12. I can assist the person to identify some goals that are specific and observable.	SA A NS D SD
13. I can assist the person to specify at least one next step that might be taken toward the goal.	SA A NS D SD

ASSESSING PEER INVOLVEMENT AND INTERVENTION

While it is important to know and assess what we are doing in a helping relationship, it is just as important to know whether or not this relationship and the intervention is making a difference. Are you accomplishing the desired outcomes? Is the person being helped to reach the goal? How can you tell?

USING ASSESSMENT PROCEDURES

Effective evaluation requires a statement of goals. Before any meaningful evaluation can take place, it is important that the goals or objectives be clearly identified. These goals tell us what we are trying to do and form the basis of any subsequent planning or procedures that might be used.

Goals may be stated in general or specific terms. *General goals* are global and focus on an overall objective. A general goal might be: "to help people feel more positively about themselves." *Specific goals*, on the other hand, usually focus on a particular behavior. For instance: "to help people identify and list three positive characteristics of themselves." Specific goals are easier to assess. In addition, perhaps the accomplishment of a series of specific goals will lead to obtaining a general goal.

Effective evaluation also requires the use of a valid measuring instrument. Once the goals are clearly defined, how do you measure the progress that has been made? If our evaluation is to have any meaning at all, then we must think how we will collect the data or information that will help us make a decision about our progress. Usually, this involves the development of some kind of questionnaire, checklist or some other form of measurement.

There are many different forms that can be used. Some have been developed by industry and commercial companies, while others are hand-made and designed specifically for a particular situation.

Evaluation is most effective when it is planned and continuous. If you have a specific plan that is organized and directed to accomplish a goal, then it is easier to evaluate. When such a plan is lacking, then goals are sometimes unclear and difficult to assess.

Evaluation also requires a positive attitude. If you view evaluation as a threat, aimed at discovering your weaknesses and spotlighting your problems, then it will not be very helpful. If seen positively, evaluation can help you improve your work. It can help you emphasize your strengths.

METHODS OF EVALUATION

There are many different approaches to assessment and evaluation. Here are some ways to evaluate your work:

The "what have I been doing" method.

In this case the emphasis is on your process—the activities techniques and strategies used. The evaluation tends to be a recording of things done. For example, you might meet ten times with an individual and during that time keep a daily log of the activities. This method provides an overall view of your work, but it is limited in terms of evaluating outcomes.

The "what do others think" method. In this method the emphasis is upon the opinions of others. You may ask people you've worked with or you might seek "objective" opinions of those who have seen or heard of your work. For example, you can use this method when you play a tape recording of an interview for your trainer. Then, your trainer makes suggestions and offers opinions about your effectiveness. Some criteria or rationale is usually behind the conclusions. It is most helpful when this criteria is outlined in advance.

The "how do I compare" method.

Comparisons can be made between one group and another or between individuals. For example, if some elementary school students were having trouble in adjusting to school, and this group were divided between those who received peer intervention and those who did not, then it would be possible to compare the progress of the two groups. If the peer intervention group seemed to make more adjustments than the other group, then it might be concluded that peer intervention was effective.

The "what happened before-and-after" method.

This method can be most effective in your work, even though it also has some limitations. In this case it is important to obtain some *baseline data* before peer intervention begins. In one situation, junior high school students were asked to complete an *Attitude About School Inventory* (baseline data). After they met with two peer co-leaders for a period of ten weeks, twice a week, the inventory was re-administered. It was then possible to compare the progress that had been made, using the before-and-after method. Because this particular method is easy to use in your work, let's take a closer look and see how it can be approached in a systematic way.

THE SYSTEMATIC CASE STUDY

No matter whether it be an individual or group, the first step in a systematic case approach is to collect some beginning (baseline) data. You may want to ask yourself: "Where are we now and how can I tell?"

To help you collect this information, you might consider the use of "self-reports"—information from the people with whom you are working. Self-reports might consist of a questionnaire, an incomplete sentence form, an autobiography, a "How I see Myself" checklist, logs, diaries, weekly calendars and so forth.

Information from outside observers might be similar. For example, students may fill out questionnaires about themselves regarding their attitudes in school. This is a self-report. A teacher might be asked to fill out the same questionnaire regarding these same students. This is a similar report, but from an independent source. A comparision might be made between the two.

After you collect baseline information, then the peer intervention begins. This may consist of individual interviews, group meetings or any other kind of activity you feel is appropriate.

Following the completion of your work, the same questionnaires or self-reports are then re-administered and a comparison is made of the before and after data.

Table V
THE SYSTEMATIC CASE STUDY

1. Identify the person or group with whom you plan to work.

(A) What is the problem?

(B) What are your goals?

2. Collect "baseline data" on the person or group.

(A) Where are you starting from?

(B) How can you tell?

For example:
Self-reports by students
Teacher reports and rating forms
School records
Observations of behavior
Parent questionnaire

3. Plan and carry out the intervention.

(A) What are you going to do? Record your activities so that you can tell what you did.

(B) When, how, where and so on did the interview take place?

4. Collect "post data" on the person or group.

(A) Where are you now?

(B) How can you tell?

5. Write a report which describes the case.

(A) The problem or goal

(B) Instruments used

(C) The intervention—describe your role and procedures

(D) Tell the results

(E) Follow-up done, if appropriate

Sometimes your work will not allow you to assess the outcomes easily. For instance, there will probably be many occasions when you are talking with someone and you realize that you can facilitate the discussion by being a good listener, clarifying ideas and identifying the important feelings that are present.

The helping process can be an integrated part of your daily living. It is not always a scheduled activity. In times like these, you will not be as concerned with evaluation, unless you have an opportunity to follow up on the situation.

However, when you know that you are assigned to work with a persons or a group, you may want to give more attention to assessing your efforts.

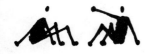

SELF-EVALUATION

PURPOSE:

To provide a means of clarifying and reinforcing what you have gained from a particular activity/experience—a means of achieving closure.

MATERIALS:

Notes to Myself, pencil/pen.

PROCEDURE:

(1) After any activity that you do in class and/or any experience that you have, write some of the following statements in your *Notes to Myself.*

> A. *I learned that I. . . .*
>
> B. *I relearned that I. . . .*
>
> C. *I realized that I. . . .*
>
> D. *I was displeased that I. . . .*
>
> E. *I discovered that I. . . .*
>
> F. *I wonder. . . .*

(2) *Share your responses with the class or pair up with another person and discuss your reactions.*

Activity 7.2:
WHAT MAKES SUCCESS?

PURPOSE:

To focus on some positive aspects of yourself; to share accomplishments and to practice listening.

MATERIALS:

Pieces of $8^1/2$ x 11-inch paper, pencil/pen.

PROCEDURE:

(1) Divide your paper by drawing a vertical line down the center.

(2) Title the left column "Accomplishments." Title the right column "Action."

(3) Now, in order, list the following in the "Accomplishments" column:

> A. One thing you accomplished while in elementary school.

> B. One thing you accomplished while in junior high or middle school.

> C. One thing you have accomplished recently.

> D. One thing you hope to accomplish in the near future.

(4) Examine each of your accomplishments. Think about what you did to be successful. There were probably many small things that contributed to your success. Write two behaviors or actions that helped you achieve each of your accomplishments.

(5) After your list is complete, form a small group and share your accomplishments. Then, tell what actions contributed to each success.

(6) After everyone has shared, discuss your reactions. Share your thoughts about such things as:

> A. What general themes did you hear?

> B. Were some of the actions the same?

> C. Are your past accomplishments related to what you hope to accomplish in the future?

PLANNING A CASE STUDY

PURPOSE:

To practice the steps involved in planning a case study.

MATERIALS:

Paper, pencil/pen.

PROCEDURE:

(1) Form a group of three.

(2) Turn to *Table V* (page 160) in this chapter, *The Systematic Case Study*.

(3) As a group, decide upon an imaginary person or group of people that you would like to help.

(4) Cooperatively, plan a systematic case study for that person or group. Be sure to give attention to each part of the study: baseline data, intervention and so forth.

(5) After your group has developed a plan, share it with another group. This group will help you critique your efforts.

(6) Make a list of three things that would be needed before you could put the plan into action.

Chapter VIII

Those who bring sunshine to the lives of others cannot keep it from themselves.

getting ready to help others

The opportunity for you to work with other people is almost here. As a peer facilitator, you soon will be spending a part of each week reaching out and caring for others. Truly, this opportunity has the potential of being one of the most meaningful and exciting times of your life! Helping others and assisting them in their search for personal meaning and worth is a special kind of work. It requires the timely use of such skills and techniques as those presented earlier.

This chapter focuses on some practical aspects of being a peer facilitator. The following will describe three peer facilitator roles. Some of the settings in which you might work will also be mentioned, as well as some examples of other peer facilitators and their work.

PEER FACILITATOR ROLES

In general, there are at least three roles that you can be involved in as a peer facilitator. While all the skills you have been practicing are related to all of these roles, there are some basic differences. Each varies according to: (1) the primary focus of the role and (2) the number of students with whom you work.

TUTOR

You may choose to be a special tutor. In general, a tutor is assigned to one or two students. The primary focus is upon helping students learn academic skills.   Tutoring may be requested in order to encourage and support a student with specific learning disabilities. Also, a student who has been absent for an extended period of time may need extra help in order to "catch up" with the rest of the class.

Being a tutor is perhaps the main way in which peer facilitators work to assist individuals in their academic achievement. Many of the students who are seen by their parents and teachers as "underachievers" will respond very favorably to the focused attention and caring relationship given by a trained tutor.

This role provides students with a non-threatening atmosphere in which to ask questions about areas that they do not understand. Thus, students who would rarely raise their hands in front of thirty other students, or who would never go up to a teacher after class and ask for help, now have a time when they can comfortably ask questions about their school assignments.

Whatever the reason for tutoring, this role is viewed by many educators and parents as one of the most vital that a peer facilitator can fulfill. With teachers having to work with more and more students—many of whom have special needs—tutoring is a means by which more students can receive needed attention and assistance.

BIG BROTHER/SISTER

A second role that you might choose is that of a "Big Brother/-Big Sister." In this role you are paired with a student who needs more attention and a trusting relationship. Here the primary focus is upon personal-social and emotional needs. While academic progress might also be of concern, personal development is of particular importance. For many students, the showing of care and concern by another person is exactly what they need. From such nurturance, they blossom.

GROUP DISCUSSION LEADER

Being a group discussion leader is a third role often assumed by peer facilitators. A group leader will usually work with five to ten students and will promote group involvement. The usual focus of discussion is centered upon enhancing the personal and social development of the group members.

Because working with more than one student at a time is demanding, some peer facilitators prefer to work as a "team" and co-lead groups. On other occasions, they also assist counselors in group counseling and guidance sessions.

As a group leader, you help select a topic and/or activity for discussion and give directions to the group members regarding the activity. You act as a catalyst for getting the group to share their thoughts and feelings with each other. You also assist them in summarizing ideas and key issues.

It is sometimes possible to combine the three roles, although a facilitator usually selects one for particular attention. Take some time and explore which role you want to fulfill. One consideration in making your selection is: *In which role will you feel most comfortable and relaxed?*

PEER FACILITATORS AND ACADEMICS

Most parents want their children to do well in school. Many feel that their child's future is dependent upon early school experiences. Also, many educators and psychologists feel that what people do in school greatly influences their self-concepts. Since school is a dominant force during the developmental years, it is no wonder that the daily happenings experienced at school play a vital role in developing attitudes, values and self-concepts. One of your primary responsibilities as a peer facilitator will be to promote academic development.

Let's take a look at some of the ways in which the three roles described earlier can be implemented. We'll look at this from both the standpoint of working with one student and/or a group of students.

JAMES' OTHER WORLD

James was in the first grade and a source of dismay to his teacher. He was not a "discipline problem;" rather, he was just the opposite. Rarely speaking to anyone else in class, James would sit quiety at his table with three other students. He never participated in any classroom activities. He seemed to be in another world.

The quality of his work had dropped from the year before. At the end of kindergarten, he had been able to count to twenty-five, say the alphabet and perform a number of other similar tasks. A few months later, it seemed as if he had forgotten everything. Also, he was not interacting and playing with the other children as he had done before. The teacher requested that James be assigned a peer facilitator.

Kathleen was a senior in high school and a member of the peer facilitator class. She was active in different activities, including student government, Spanish Club and the Boosters. She thought that someday she might want to be an elementary school teacher, but she had no experience in working with children. She wondered if she could talk with little children and wasn't sure what to say. But, after hearing about James and his problem, Kathleen decided she would try to work with him. She arranged a conference with his teacher.

In the beginning, progress was slow. Kathleen went to James' class three times a week and spent approximately an hour each visit. She wanted to establish a trusting, comfortable relationship with him before attempting to accomplish anything else. Since he was hesitant, at first, to talk when they were alone, Kathleen decided to spend time helping James in the classroom while he was with his classmates.

She even assisted some of the others in the class in order to help James see that it was okay to talk and work with her. They also spent some time playing on the playground, making puppets and even eating lunch together. Kathleen worked hard to help James feel more comfortable with her. After three to four weeks, her efforts began to pay off.

First, the teacher noticed that James was interacting more with his classmates. In fact, he was even developing a "buddy" in the room—something that he had made no attempt to do before. Also, the teacher became aware of his increased participation in classroom activiites and he completed assignments. He was now raising his hand on occasion, was turning in more of his work and once again was able to say the alphabet and count.

By the time Kathleen left the school, both she and the teacher were proud of James and his progress. He still had a lot of catching up to do, but he was now making an effort and he appeared much happier in school.

Kathleen said: "I worried, at first, whether James would like me and I wondered if he would even talk. It wasn't easy, but when I learned that he looked forward to seeing me, I began to have more hope and I gained more confidence. It was really great when the teacher told me that I had been of help to James. You know, I'm going to miss spending time with him."

JERRY'S ACCIDENT

Steve was also a member of Kathleen's peer facilitator class. He became interested when he learned that it was a class that helped people work with people and that he could learn more about communicating with others.

Steve liked sports and he was considering coaching as a career. Even though he had experienced some success in athletics and was popular, he was shy. Sometimes others would tease him about it. He laughed with them, but it made him wonder if he would ever be able to coach others. He knew that he could learn more about himself, as well as learn more "talking" skills.

With some encouragement from others, Steve decided to join the class. It was during the second semester of the school year that Steve met Jerry.

Jerry, a tenth grader, had missed six weeks of school because of a car wreck. Once he returned to school, it became evident that he had fallen behind in all of his classes. . . especially math and science. Since college was part of his future, Jerry felt pressured and anxious to catch up.

Jerry's teachers wanted to help, but they had already given a lot of time to Jerry. Jerry's math teacher recognized that he needed more individual help, so she suggested that a peer facilitator work with him.

Jerry met with Steve three times a week during their lunch hour. Steve made a special effort to talk with Jerry's teachers. He also got make-up assignments and worksheets for him to do. Their sessions went well and, after five weeks, Jerry felt that he could make it on his own.

Jerry was grateful to Steve for his time and effort and Steve was pleased too. Both had found a new friend.

WE'RE NOT DOING TOO WELL. . . .

Dick, Alice, Sharon, Pete and Dawn, all middle school students, were referred to the guidance office because of their lack of interest and success in school. Their aptitude test scores indicated that they had the potential to make better grades; yet, all of them were struggling to pass at least two of their classes. All were getting pressure from their parents to do better. They wanted to improve their grades. Derrick and Jan, two peer facilitators, co-led a group composed of these five students.

In their peer facilitator class, Derrick and Jan had experienced a number of small group activities. After reviewing their *Notes About Me* notebooks, they talked about the activities that they might use. They wanted some structured group experiences that would help the students to think about themselves; to focus on their attitudes about school; and to be more aware of what they were doing in their classes. Derrick thought that it would be important for the group to listen to each others' ideas about school, rather than to begin immediately with some attention to study skills. Jan agreed, but she also thought it would be important to help the students change their study habits through some course of action.

After discussing some possible activities, they developed a general plan that eventually led to a specific technique which would help the individual members of the group improve their grades.

At the first meeting, the two facilitators outlined the major purposes of the group. After some introductory activities aimed at helping the participants relax, the group began to share ideas. They talked about their lack of achievemernt. Future personal goals and aspirations were also discussed and then related to school. What were the students doing to help or hinder achievement of their goals?

After ten group sessions (two sessions per week), the facilitators then assisted the group members to write individual "contracts." These were designed to promote more commitments and to get them to do something about their grades. Pete's contract is an example:

> *I, Pete, being the wise and determined young man that I am, hereby do swear to accomplish the following:*
>
> *A. Study 45 minutes each evening of the week.*
>
> *B. Finish and hand in at least 80% of all my homework.*
>
> *C. Study in a quiet place.*
>
> *D. Get a written report from each of my teachers on Fridays concerning my efforts for the week.*
>
> *Accomplishing the above will result in my being able to go skateboarding on the weekends.*
>
> *Signed Pete*

After completing their contracts, each participant negotiated with the other members of the group concerning who would co-sign their contracts. A co-signer agreed to serve as a "support system" and consented to periodically meet and check on the person. The facilitators and participants agreed to meet again at the end of the grading period to share results of their efforts and celebrate accomplishments.

PEER FACILITATORS AND PERSONAL-SOCIAL DEVELOPMENT

Along with the responsibility of promoting academic development, schools are becoming more responsible for the personal-social needs of students. Much of the research done in the areas of education and psychology clearly points out the importance of students' self-concepts in relation to their efforts to succeed academically.

Books such as Purkey's *Self-Concept and School Achievement* and Rosenthal's *Pygmalion in the Classroom* are based upon the premise that how we feel about ourselves has a very dramatic bearing upon our ability to do well in school.

You can enhance the personality development and self-concepts of other students. Through a variety of activities, strategies and skills, you can become an integral part of your school's efforts to encourage social and personal growth. Since you will spend about five to six hours of each day—for approximatley 180 days each year—in school interacting with other students, it makes sense to prepare you to be a care-giver and support system for others.

MARY ANN'S DILEMMA

Mary Ann was a friendly, active and intelligent fifth grade student—a "winner" at whatever she attempted. She had lots of friends, was involved in a number of extra-curricular activities (such as swimming and music) and still managed to make A's and B's on her report card. She cared deeply for both her parents. Her only regret about her family was that there were no other brothers or sisters with whom she could play.

Then, it happened. Her father took her aside one day and began explaining that he would be moving to an apartment across town. He continued by saying: "Your mother and I are getting a divorce." He explained that they no longer wanted to live together, but that they both still loved Mary Ann and didn't want to hurt her. Much of the conversation was lost in the sobbing and pain that engulfed Mary, as the reality of the situation hit her.

In the weeks that followed, everyone who knew Mary Ann noticed how quiet and withdrawn she had become. The girl, who had smiled, laughed and danced a lot, now spent most of her time alone—sad and confused over her parents' divorce.

In desperation, Mary Ann's mother called the counselor at the elementary school and pleaded that "something must be done to break Mary Ann's depression." After consulting with Mary Ann's teacher and mother, the counselor decided that a high school peer facilitator might be effective. Thus, Beth came into Mary Ann's life.

The following weeks were a struggle, both for Mary Ann and Beth. At first, Mary Ann rejected all of Beth's efforts to make friends. She continued to do poorly in school. Most of her afternoons and weekends were spent in her room listening to the radio, reading books or writing in her diary. Finally, Beth was able to get Mary Ann to agree to go swimming with her. The afternoon was spent getting to know each other. Then, Beth surprised her with a picnic at the park.

As the weeks passed, Mary Ann came to trust Beth. They worked on Mary Ann's homework, planted a "garden" in a box and watched the seeds turn into plants. They even went to a movie or two. Slowly, Mary Ann began to talk about her feelings of anger and fear. She spoke of confusion and hurt. Beth did her best to help Mary Ann face the reality that her father was not going to return home.

By the end of the year, going to school was once more a pleasure for Mary Ann. Her friends were coming to her house to play again and she was able to accept her mother's new life style. She and Beth have remained friends for three years— even though Beth is now in college—and they still communicate with each other.

I'M NEW HERE. . . .

Kevin was new to the high school, having transferred during January of his senior year. He wondered how he would "fit in." He soon found that the classes were somewhat different from those he had been taking. Concerned and frustrated, he made an appointment with his counselor. After the two of them explored the situation, it was decided that Kevin would be introduced to Nick.

This was Nick's second year as a peer facilitator. Nick was well known around the school for his sense of humor and leadership. It was hoped that Nick could introduce Kevin around the school, spend some lunch time talking with him and discuss Kevin's progress in school.

When Nick was contacted about helping Kevin adjust to the school, Nick readily agreed. A schedule of meeting times was worked out and Nick begain introducing Kevin to some of his friends. He also did some tutoring with Kevin regarding his research writing project.

After a couple of weeks, Kevin made another appointment with his counselor. At this session, Kevin said he was much more comfortable and felt more "accepted." He talked about some girls who interested him. Kevin also mentioned that he was going to try out for the baseball team.

During the last week of school, Nick received a personal note from Kevin thanking him for his help. Both had made a new friend; both learned a little more about the process of adjusting to a new situation.

A SELF-AWARENESS LAB

While there are times when a one-to-one approach is needed, many times peer facilitators are involved in developmental tasks with groups of students. A group approach allows peers to have an impact on many more students than could be achieved by working with only one individual at a time. It also creates a more realistic setting in which to talk. Groups provide students with a safe place in which to "try out" new attitudes, beliefs and behaviors. One such developmental group approach is the *Self-Awareness Lab.*

Peer facilitators can co-lead a lab which consists of a series of structured group experiences. The activities assist the students (approximatley seven to nine) to develop self-awareness, communications skills and an ability to make decisions. Generally, the members of these labs have volunteered to participate. Teachers occasionally recommend students for the experience.

Karen and Roger were two peer facilitators who were assigned to a middle school. They agreed to lead a group of students, twice a week, for a period of three weeks. After reviewing their peer facilitator class experiences and notes, they decided to develop their own *Self-Awareness Lab.* Their planning notes for the six sessions follow:

Session 1

1. Introduce ourselves and quickly describe the purpose of the group. The purpose: To learn more about ourselves and others as well as develop some communication skills.

2. Learn everyone's name by playing *The Name Game*.

3. Groundrules:

   (A) Talk one at a time.

   (B) Listen carefully so that you can remember what others say.

   (C) Everyone has the right "to pass."

4. Go-round: To get them talking, start a "Go-round." Each person shares: *Three Things I Enjoy Doing*.

5. Activity: *Design An Ideal School*

Ask questions like:

   (A) What rules would you have?

   (B) How would you decide who could teach there?

   (C) What characteristics would a teacher have to have?

   (D) How many hours a day would you go?

   (E) Tell how a typical class would be taught?

   (F) What about tests and grades?

Session 2

1. Begin by reminding the group of the groundrules.

2. Go-round: "Name one person that you respect and/or admire. Tell the group your reasons for feeling as you do."

3. Activity: *Rank Ordering Priorities*

4. Share individual responses and discuss how the people came to choose their responses.

5. Summarize key points of today's session.

Session 3

1. Begin with *The IALAC Story* (2.3). Discuss.

2. If time, have them list *Fifteen Things I Love to Do* (2.2).

Session 4

1. Begin with *Twenty Questions* (3.1) for ten minutes.

2. Activity: *Unfinished Sentences* (2.1).

3. Share responses in pairs, then discuss as a group.

Session 5

1. Begin with Go-round topic: "What are two or three things that confuse you about life?

2. Activity: Discuss the following quote by Oscar Wilde:

"To LIVE is the rarest thing in the world. Most people EXIST. . . that is all."

3. Summarize and clarify the comments.

Session 6

1. Begin with the activity: *Positive Feedback* (5.1)

2. Have group fill out group evaluation form.

3. Go-round: Each person makes one statement beginning with any of the following:

" I learned that I. . . ."

"I relearned that I. . . ."

"I wonder. . . ."

"I hope that I. . . ."

These statements will reflect the happenings of the six group meetings.

A COMMUNICATIONS LAB

Later in the year, Karen and Roger decided to organize a communications lab for some other students. It's not enough to be aware of self; it is important to know how to communicate that awareness in a socially effective way.

Communication labs can be organized in a number of different ways. Almost all of them, however, have the following ingredients:

1. Learning to be a better listener by tuning in to others' ideas and feelings;

2. Learning to respond to ideas and feelings;

3. Learning to give praise;

4. Learning to take a stand and to confront others; and

5. Practicing the facilitative skills, both in and out of the group.

The lab has a positive focus, even though at one point some attention is given to telling others about unpleasant feelings at times. Here is a plan that Karen and Roger used:

LAB SCHEDULE

Session 1: Beginning the Group

Introduction—

Begin by asking the group about the different kinds of groups in which they have been. Explain that this is a special kind of learning group and probably it will be different from other small groups they may have been in.

Activity I—

Group member introductions. Group members get into pairs. Ask them to interview one another for about three minutes each. Then, have the members introduce their partners to the rest of the group. Encourage questions. Practice saying names— maybe use *The Name Game.*

Activity II—

Listening for feelings. After some discussion about the importance of feelings, pantomine some feeling words and let the members guess.

Introduce Groundrules—(put on chart)

1. We talk about our feelings and thoughts.

2. We listen to how others are feeling and thinking.

3. We respect the right of anyone to "pass."

4. We talk for ourselves and to each other—use "you" and "I."

5. We keep what is said in the group confidential.

Session 2: Self-Disclosure

Review—

Go around the circle and members name each other again. Ask for any reactions to the last sessions.

Activity—

Self-Disclosing Shield. Each group member draws a coat of arms or shield on a sheet of paper. The shield is then divided into four equal parts and numbers put in each part. Have the members of the group draw a symbol in each of the parts for the following:

(A) Something you would most like to do someday.

(B) Something you don't like about school.

(C) Something you like about your family

(D) Something you are good at right now.

Members then share at least one of the symbols with the group. Leaders too!

Session 3: Self-Disclosure and Feedback

Activity—

Secret Pooling. Members write three words that they think their classmates would probably use to describe them. They also write three words that they would use to describe themselves. Collect and shuffle the papers. Then, read each paper aloud, one at a time. Members try to guess whose descriptions are being read. After guessing, ask what other words might be added to some people's lists.

Session 4: Feedback

Activity—

Indirect Feedback. Members describe each other through using metaphors. The following model may be helpful: "(Student's name) I see you as a (object)." Members should provide as much detail as possible—color, size, materials, where the object is found, who owns it and so forth. Feelings toward the object should also be a part of the feedback.

Session 5: Unstructured Session

Activity—

Open. This session will be left often for whatever special needs arise in the group. Possible activities might be role playing, communication triads, values clarification and free discussion.

Session 6: Termination and Positive Statements

Activity—

Strength Bombardment. Each member takes a turn sitting in the middle of the circle while other members tell the person sitting in the center what they see as that individual's best quality or strength in communicating with other people. Every member gives one or more positive quality. While receiving feedback, that person cannot respond. After all have been in the center, reactions and questions take place.

Evaluation—

Questionnaire. Members can fill out a group evaluation form:

1. The group increased my understanding of self.   SA A NS D SD
2. The group increased my understanding of others.   SA A NS D SD
3. The group affected my behavior outside the group.   SA A NS D SD
4. I would recommend the group to others.   SA A NS D SD
5. What I liked best about the group was. . . .
6. What I liked least about the group was. . . .

OTHER PERSONAL-SOCIAL GROUP ACTIVITIES

The use of the *Developing Understanding of Self and Others (DUSO)* kit with small groups of elementary students has become increasingly popular with peer facilitators. This kit of structured activities includes puppets, stories, cassette tapes and illustrated posters. Also provided is a training manual with suggestions for using the materials in the kit. Peer facilitators can use the kit as a vehicle for stimulating discussion concerning such topics as: friends, sharing, the importance of listening and so forth.

Another program that has been used with elementary school students is called the *Magic Circle*, which consists of a series of small group discussions that helps students talk about themselves and others. The program outlines different topics to discuss. Peer facilitators can select some of the topics, organize them into a meaningful sequence and provide the young students with an interesting experience.

"*Feelings classes*" is another group approach that has been used effectively by peer facilitators. Feelings classes are a set of structured group experiences that help students learn more about human behavior and how feelings and behaviors are related.

The major objectives of a feelings class are:

(1) *To help students become aware that feelings exist.* This involves a sensitizing experience. Only after students are sensitized to their feelings, can they learn to effectively deal with them. In many cases, this means teaching young children more about feeling words and helping them build a vocabulary that will allow them to express themselves more.

(2) *To help students become aware that people possess all kinds of feelings.* Students need to learn that they have many feelings in common with other students and that they are not alone in their experiences. It is reassuring to learn that others also feel the same way, at times. This reduces feelings of inadequacy and guilt.

(3) *To help students become more aware that feelings are neither bad nor ugly.* People do not have to act out their feelings. All of us learn to inhibit certain behaviors or channel certain feelings into socially acceptable ways. There is no need to ignore or deny what we are feeling. That only leads to ineffective thinking and deceptive behaviors.

(4) *To help students learn socially effective ways of expressing feelings.* Because the expression of some feelings is socially unacceptable, it is important to learn ways that these feelings can be channeled. Those feelings exist, so what do we do with them?

Helping young children to identify their feelings of dissappointment, anger or jealousy, and giving them the opportunity to explore ways of dealing with those feelings, can enhance personal growth and development. It leads to more responsible young citizens.

Feelings classes can be organized around a 20 to 45 minute time block. In almost every situation, an interesting and stimulating activity is used that encourages the participants to think about feelings and behaviors. For example, the issue of friendship might be the general theme that sets the state for a series of activities.

PEER FACILITATORS AND CAREER DEVELOPMENT

All students have an interest in choosing a job or career. Teachers and parents often stress the importance of "looking to the future" as young people progress through school. Pressures associated with making a career decision increase as students move toward graduation.

Most school systems use standardized tests as one way of gathering information about the abilities and aptitudes of their students. Peer facilitators can be trained to help other students get the most out of their test results.

Here's an example of one approach:

AMY'S APTITUDES: PLANNING FOR THE FUTURE

Amy was in the tenth grade. She had mixed feelings concerning school. On the one hand, she wanted to do her best and please her parents, but then again she was confused and unsure about what she wanted to do with her life. She was getting tired of being told: "You'd better prepare for your future and get an education." She couldn't even decide what type of future she wanted. At times, much of her school work seemed a waste of time.

Amy and her tenth grade class took the *Differential Aptitude Test (DAT)*—a standardized test designed to measure a person's potential for occupational areas. She had tried hard on the test because her counselor had said that it could help her begin to choose a career.

Amy received the test results during her social studies class. The counselors used some peer facilitators to assist them in explaining the results. Amy found herself sitting in a group with five other classmates and a peer facilitator.

A counselor made some general statements concerning the *DAT* and how to understand the results. Then, the peer facilitator began to lead the group through a series of activities designed to increase more understanding of test scores. Amy shared what she thought was important in a job. She also had an opportunity to compare her scores with the scores of persons who were already employed and successful in certain areas.

After exploring the meaning of her results and looking at other factors related to her career choice, Amy was more confident about what she needed to do. While she still had not discovered the one special career that was for her, she realized that she wanted to work with people. In addition, she had become more aware of her next steps—making some phone calls and changing the classes that she had scheduled for the next year.

As a result of her experience in the peer-led *DAT* discussion group, Amy felt she had taken some positive steps toward knowing what she wanted to do. The importance of certain school subjects was more obvious and she now felt the excitement of having a goal she wanted to achieve. Amy was on her way!

THE VOCATIONAL EXPLORATION GROUP (VEG)

There are a number of other ways in which peer facilitators assist in career exploration. Sometimes they work in the guidance office, reviewing materials and discussing common interests and problems with students. At other times they might work with a counselor on a career project designed to provide more career information. Sometimes they lead discussion groups.

One such group that might be used is the *Vocational Exploration Group (VEG)*. At this time the *VEG* is being used almost exclusively by certified counselors. Only limited use has been made by peers as leaders. However, one experimental program in Georgia has indicated that peer facilitators can use the *VEG* with effectiveness.

Briefly, the *VEG* is a small group experience for about five to six students. The group leader follows a trainer manual that outlines the procedures and tells the leader what to say. By following the manual, a peer facilitator can lead a group through a series of procedures and tasks. These help the participants explore their job interests, examine the way in which the world of work is organized and take a next step.

No attempt is made to tell others what they should do or what might be best for them. Because it is sequential and outlined in a trainer manual, the *VEG* is an ideal exploration program that can be used by peer facilitators.

OTHER PEER FACILITATOR SETTINGS

Peer facilitators are needed wherever there are human beings. Alternative settings are almost endless. Here are some that may be of interest to you. The list is not inclusive of all the possibilities.

RETIREMENT CENTERS

The number of elderly persons who need someone with whom to talk and relate is increasing. The hours spent talking and reminiscing with the elderly have provided some meaningful moments to peer facilitators.

RUNAWAY SHELTERS

There are many teenagers who choose to "hit the road." Peer facilitators can play a part in the individual and group counseling sessions held at these centers. Having other young people with whom to relate is often one key to breaking down a runaway's hostility and fear.

HOSPITALS

Our nation's hospitals are filled with frightened children and lonely adults who want someone to spend time with them. Peers can serve as an integral part of the treatment given to many hospital patients.

JUVENILE SHELTERS

Some young people have been incarcerated in a local place of detention. They often feel alienated from others and can use the help of peer facilitators to think about their situation. This might be done as a part of a recreational activity or as a scheduled helping interview.

SPECIAL EDUCATION CLASSES

Peers have been a part of the efforts to provide the maximum school experience for educationally handicapped and learning disabled students. Some peer facilitators work with special education units, while others offer tutoring or serve as "teacher aides" in regular classes where special education students have been mainstreamed.

IN-SCHOOL SUSPENSION ROOMS

Many schools are now providing "time-out" rooms for students who are having difficulties with a class or teacher. Rather than suspend or expel a student, the person goes to the time-out room. It is here that a peer facilitator might be assigned to meet and talk with that student. Sometimes it is helpful to facilitate people to "blow off steam" and then to help them think more about their situation.

WHAT OTHER PEER FACILITATORS HAVE SAID

When some veteran peer facilitators were asked what they would suggest to others who are interested in being facilitators, this is what they shared:

SHANNON:

"This class requires a lot of concentration. Rather than dwell on what else is happening in your life, put your energies into the class activities so that you can learn faster."

ROGER:

"Being a peer facilitator is serious business. I take a lot of pride in my work. It's work that you can be proud of. . . when you give of yourself and help others. It's a wonderful feeling !"

RONNIE:

"Learning how to respond to others is one of the most important skills that can be learned. It effects everything else that you do and it takes commitment. Words are powerful and it's important to think before speaking out."

KAY:

"Being involved and committed is what counts. I've enjoyed helping others and I've learned a lot too. Practicing the skills of listening and responding is important if you are going to be successful. It may feel funny at first—new ways of talking—but it sure pays off when working with others. It's also affected my own life. The more I practice, the more the skills seems to be a part of me."

FELICIA:

"Sharing yourself with others is important. I learned more about gentleness and acceptance through the program. It wasn't so important whether I agreed or disagreed with others, as much as trying to "tune in" to the person. I learned that some people just march to the tune of a different drummer than I do—and that's okay."

JOAN:

"I had to plan in order to be successful. Taking things for granted and just showing up is a sure way to fail. When I was unprepared, I felt anxious; but when I had an idea of what might happen, I felt more confident."

TRISH:

"I learned that you can care about people, but if you don't respond to them in some way, they will never know it. What is most surprising is that by being a good listener and trying to respond in a facilitative way, I found that it was easy to care about others. My caring for others has increased."

ROBBIE:

"You can't daydream when working with others. It's embarrassing to everyone if you get caught. You can't just sit back and relax. Being a good facilitator is work."

PAT:

"Peer class is a different kind of class. You get out of it what you put into it. It's a type of class that depends upon the other students. There's no real set answer for some of the problems that come up."

KAREN:

"You've got to have an open mind if you're going to be a peer facilitator—that's for sure. There are a lot of different opinions about everything. If you are close-minded, people won't trust you. I learned that you don't have to agree with anyone about anything, but you can respect their rights and try to understand their position more. It helps."

CYNTHIA:

"If you want to be successful, you've got to get involved. Don't just sit around and let everyone else do things, even if you're not sure at first. It gets easier as the class goes along. While it is serious, you can have a lot of fun, too!

LAVERNE:

"Facilitating people isn't a game. If you think that it is, or maybe that it's just a way of manipulating people, then maybe you'd better think about it again. It's a lot more than what I ever expected it to be."

WARREN:

"Taking the time to plan is important. It helps you make decisions at certain times. It should be a flexible plan and not so rigid that you're forcing something on somebody."

SUSAN:

"Tuning in to what others are thinking and feeling is the key to success. It takes practice, but it is worth it."

RICK:

"Sometimes learning new things can be discouraging and you shouldn't lose hope right away. If things start to go wrong, just keep going. Talk with someone, but don't give up. You might be making progress and not even know that you are. Some people get more out of it than you realize at the time. It may be only later that they might tell you."

JUAN:

"The more time you give to this class, the more you get out of it. You can goof off or you can get with it and really learn something. This is a good time to find out about yourself—don't miss the opportunity!"

LINDA:

"You should ask yourself: 'Why am I taking this class?' If you're not committed to its objectives and the idea that you can help others, then you're going to be disappointed. Without commitment, you will never learn the meaning or the value of the class."

Activity 8.1:

PREPARING FOR YOUR FIRST ASSIGNMENT

PURPOSE:

To insure that you have planned adequately for your first experience as a peer facilitator and to assist you in building self-confidence.

MATERIALS:

None.

PROCEDURE:

(1) Know your asssignment ! Be clear on your role. What is expected of you? Obtain some general information about the person(s) with whom you will work.

(2) Answer the following questions *before* beginning your work:

A. What are the goals? What are you trying to accomplish?

B. What can the participant(s) expect to gain by cooperating with you?

C. What are two or three possible problems you may confront? How would you attempt to resolve each of these problems?

D. What are two or three activities that you feel would be appropriate for your first session? What stimulating questions can you ask?

(3) Share your ideas with a partner.

Activity 8.2:
GETTING READY

PURPOSE:

To begin planning for a peer facilitator intervention.

MATERIALS:

Notes to Myself notebook, paper and pencil/pen.

PROCEDURE:

(1) Review your *Notes to Myself* notebook, this text and any other materials that you believe will be helpful in planning an intervention.

(2) Identify your five favorite activities—activities that you would like to use with others.

(3) Review these activities; take note of the procedures and add any comments that you believe will be helpful.

(4) Next, place the activities in order (one to five) that you think would be feasible.

(5) In addition, develop some interesting questions for each of the activities. Make some notes that will help you proceed with the activity.

(6) Now, share your plan with someone else in the class. Encourage them to help you critique the plan.

(7) What three things are needed before you can put the plan (the sequence of activities) into action?

Activity 8.3:
ACCOUNTABILITY LOG

PURPOSE:

To maintain a record of your experiences as a peer facilitator; to assist you in planning.

MATERIALS:

A spiral notebook or stenographer's pad, pencil/pen.

PROCEDURE:

(1) Following each activity which you facilitate, make an entry which includes the following points:

    A. Date of activity.

    B. Time spent on activity.

    C. Who participated.

    D. Name of activity/experience.

    E. Your impressions of how the activity went.

    F. Important statements made by the participants.

    G. What you feel would be a good activity for the next meeting.

(2) Discuss your entry with another person in the class.

Chapter IX

Just because you're paranoid, it doesn't mean they're not out to get you.

problem
moments

There are going to be a lot of exciting times for you as a peer facilitator. However, you will probably experience some problem moments. Interestingly enough, if you are active in your work, you will probably experience more problems than those who are less involved. *Problems are a natural part of being involved.*

Problem moments can provide a valuable learning experience. Moreover, having a problem does not necessarily mean that you are failing. Perhaps the most important thing is the way in which you resolve some of your problems.

What follows are some problems and concerns that other peer facilitators have reported. Perhaps you will be able to avoid some of the same situations by benefiting from the experiences of others.

"Sometimes I feel "phony" when I try to facilitate others."

Facilitative responses are not common-place in our society today. It is only natural that you will initially feel a little uncomfortable when responding to others in this way. Since this is a new
way of responding, it's possible that others will experience you
as being different. However, with practice you can make the
high facilitative responses a natural part of your personality
and everyday conversation. It doesn't have to have a serious
focus every time. As long as you are honest and sincere in your
responses, your efforts will probably bring results.

*"I feel anxious when others expect me to resolve their problems
for them."*

Because of your training, you may experience people who
believe that you can provide them with "the answers" and that
you will solve their problems. They may see you as a "mini psychologist." As you know, this is not the case. You recognize, of
course, that you are limited in your training. It is important to
remember that the ultimate responsibility for the problem—
and its resolution—rests with the person you are helping. You
can only do so much. This is usually in the form of being an empathic listener, clarifying issues, helping to examine alternatives and encouraging action.

"How do I keep from taking sides?"

Friends may ask if you agree with them. Persons that you are helping may urge you to share your reactions to what they have said. When you believe that the time is appropriate, you may want to tell them your thoughts. However, there are those who will also pressure you to decide for them what is right or wrong. They will want you to make their decisions.

Try to avoid making decisions for others. Be empathic. Discuss alternatives. Your neutral position, if you can maintain one, is important. It allows people to assume more responsibility for their own lives. Remember, it is their decision and you can best help by exploring with them alternatives and consequences, leaving the final decision to them.

"I've been working with a person and I'm not seeing much progress. It's getting discouraging."

You are worried about your effectiveness. Working with people can be frustrating, especially when there isn't much evidence that you are being helpful. Maybe your expectations are too high. You really want to make a difference and yet you are "not seeing" any results.

We rarely make dramatic changes in a short period of time. Many of the problems facing people have developed over a period of years. Moreover, habits are not easy to break. It's not likely that you'll get instant results.

Be consistent. Be patient. Remember that you are planting the seeds that may not sprout or take hold for a while. Then again, sometimes growth is taking place, but you can't see what is happening.

Mark was a high school peer facilitator working with an elementary school student in a big brother role and he didn't see much result from the "fun and just talking" sessions that took place. After about eight weeks, Mark indicated that he wouldn't be coming to the school much longer. His assignment to that school was nearing an end. The little boy didn't react much.

A short time later, the boy's parents called and wondered why the sessions with Mark had to end. They reported that the boy was happier, talked more and looked forward to going to school. While in the past he had been withdrawn, now he was more active. This came as a surprise to Mark who, at times, thought he was just passing time with the boy. To the little boy and the parents' pleasure, Mark decided to meet with him some more. With some positive feedback, Mark was even more eager to be a peer facilitator.

There can be no doubt that evidence of effectiveness can be reinforcing. It's reassuring; it's motivating! Unfortunately, too many times you will not hear about the favorable impact you are having in your work.

"Because I've been trained as a peer facilitator, others sometimes expect me to be more perfect than I really am. They expect me to always be happy and understanding. What should I do?"

It is quite a burden when people expect you to "have your act together" all the time. You are a human being with conflicts in your life, just like everyone else. You are going to have problems and situations that are just as confusing to you as the problems and situations that confront those with whom you work. Occasionally, you may want to share this fact with others.

As one peer facilitator said: "Hey, everything isn't always perfect with me either. I have times when I am confused and frustrated—sometimes feeling very alone." You may want to tell about some ways in which you deal with your feelings and situations. Remember, all your problems don't have to be resolved before you can facilitate others.

"What should I do when I'm talking with someone who sees things so much differently than I, yet they want to know what I would do?"

Taking a neutral position is not always easy, especially when the person asks what you would do. To avoid answering a question may make you appear uninterested or unwilling to share ideas. If the request for your opinion comes early, you may want to delay stating your opinions for awhile Ask for more information: "Well, first, let me see if I understand your situation. You said. . . ." This may give you more opportunity to facilitate the discussion. Later, when the person says: "Okay, but what would you do?", perhaps it is time to tell them your thoughts.

For example, one peer facilitator was working with a boy who was unhappy with school. School had no meaning for him. He was thinking of quitting school during his senior year. A full-time job would give him the money he wanted and also more independence from his parents. After some discussion and after the facilitator had helped him explore alternatives, the question came: "Well, what would you do in my situation?" Clarifying, the facilitator said: "You want me to tell you what to do?" "That's right," came the response. After this clarification, the facilitator then continued: "Well, I'm not sure how I would respond in your situation because I'm not facing the same things right now. However, quitting school would not be the kind of alternative that I would choose. At least for me, finishing school would get first priority. Then, I'd probably look at some of the other things you thought of— like a part-time job."

Don't rush in with your opinions and advice. It's the *timely sharing* of your opinions and ideas that really makes the difference.

"I'm having trouble getting along with another peer who is a member of our class. I'm not sure what to do."

It must be disconcerting to hear all the things said in class about how important it is to be empathic, caring and understanding of other people, only to find yourself feeling uncomfortable with someone right next to you. There are some people who will make you feel uncomfortable. Some of the people in class are going to be uniquely different from you. You don't have to be close friends with everyone.

It is important to examine your degree of discomfort. If it affects your ability to perform in the class, then there are several things you could do. For instance:

(1) Explore the situation with your trainer. Try to discover what issues are involved.

(2) Go to the other person, sit down with that person and share your feelings of discomfort. See if you can learn more about the other person's perceptions.

(3) Meet with the trainer and the person involved to share what you can. Be honest. Try to examine the situation.

Remember, the skills you've learned are not only to be used *outside* of class.

"What do I do when I want to be understanding and accepting, yet the person I'm working with continues to break rules and get into trouble?"

The role conflict between being an empathic, understanding listener and being someone who gently confronts a person oftentimes creates this kind of confusion. You may ask yourself: "Just where do I stand; where do I draw the line?" You may be wanting to say: "Hey, you are really going to get yourself in a bind!"

If you have developed a positive relationship and you sense that a person really cares about what you think, then you can say: "Look, I am realy concerned about what I see you doing right now; it's confusing to me. I am worried about you!"

"I like many of the things we've learned in class, but now I'm more critical of others than before—especially my teachers and parents."

The study of human behavior and interpersonal relationships will make you more aware of others. It can make you more alert to some aspects of a relationship that you don't like, such as the way you interact with your parents.

One peer facilitator, Janet, complained that her parents never listened to her. She avoided them because conversations always ended in arguments. She said: "My father is worse than my mother, but they are both so old-fashioned and fixed in their ways. It is impossible to talk with them."

After some self-examination, Janet concluded that her parents, despite their age and experience, had never had an opportunity to take a class in interpersonal relationships. Even though they cared about her, their limited communication skills tended to provoke arguments more than discussions.

After more thought, Janet decided to listen more to her parents and to avoid arguing. She also decided to talk with her parents about her peer facilitator class. Instead of faulting her parents, and being disappointed because they seemed less understanding than she wanted them to be, Janet introduced and modeled her communication skills at home.

She later reported: "There is still a lot of room for improvement, but it is much better at home. At least we don't fight over little things as much and there seems to be fewer hassles."

The teaching of communications skills is a relatively new concept. There are many who have not benefited from instruction. Then again, there are those who have been exposed to the skills, but who have failed to integrate those skills into their daily lives.

"I feel like I have a lot of problems myself which need attention. When I go to work with other persons, I sometimes have trouble concentrating on their problems."

When you have been assigned a facilitator's role, it is important that you concentrate on the discussion at hand and not let your mind drift to your own problems. If you do, the others are bound to sense some distance. They may misinterpret your preoccupation with your own thoughts as rejection of them. They may think you don't care about them and are just putting in your time as part of some assignment. As you know, that would be unfortunate.

If you have a problem that is drawing upon a lot of your energies, then you may want to seek help from someone. It may be another peer facilitator with whom you feel close, or the trainer. It may be one of your school counselors. As you've learned from your reading, talking with a facilitative listener can be helpful. If the problem persists, you may need to make some adjustments in your work.

On the other hand, if your problem is not overwhelming you and it is only on occasion that you find it difficult to concentrate, then you may even want to consider sharing your thoughts with the person you are helping.

For example: "I'm having a difficult time paying attention today. I know you have been telling me about something that's important to you, but for some reason, my mind is on. . . ." It is a genuine, honest response and the person with whom you are working will probably respect you more for it. Perhaps after some brief explanation of your distraction, you can then relax and give more attention to the person with whom you are working.

SUMMARY

The skills and activities presented in the previous chapters are some ways for enhancing your effectiveness as a peer facilitator. But, no matter what the role and/or setting, one important consideration to remember is to be genuine—be yourself! *Learn to trust your inner knowledge, using the skills the best way that you can. Let your natural caring and gentleness come out.*

Your caring and sharing, combined with your facilitative skills, can make a difference in people's lives.

HOW I HANDLE MY PROBLEMS

PURPOSE:

To explore past experiences in resolving problems.

MATERIALS:

Pencil/pen.

PROCEDURE:

(1) Think about some problem situations which have confronted you during the past year.

(2) Fill in the following chart:

Problems I Have Had	How I Attempted to Resolve the Problem	The Final Outcome
1.		
2.		
3.		

(3) Complete the following unfinished sentences:

    A. When confronted with a major problem, I....

    B. My problems are usually caused by....

    C. In order to become more successful at resolving my problems, I need to....

(4) Share your responses in trios.

Activity 9.2:

WHAT SHOULD BE DONE NOW?

PURPOSE:

To examine some problem moments that other facilitators have had; to explore alternatives.

MATERIALS:

The following problem moments, paper, pencil/pen.

PROCEDURE:

(1) Read a problem moment from the following list. Imagine what you would do if you were in this situation.

(2) Write a response that illustrates what you might do first, then next and so on. If it is a response, then put quotation marks around your words.

(3) Get in a small group and have someone read a problem moment aloud. Then each person in the group tells what they would do. Be sure to read or say your response aloud.

PROBLEM MOMENTS:

(1) Dale was a junior high school student who liked meeting with you. Your individual conferences have been going well and this is the fifth time you have met with him. Everything seemed to be moving along slowly, when suddenly Dale began to talk about some of the problems he was having on the school bus.

Some boys have been teasing him. He tried to ignore them, then to laugh it off, but the teasing has become more hostile and the insults more painful. He says: "I'm scared; tonight they are going to get me again. I don't know what to do. They just keep picking and picking and picking. The worst part is that nobody else seems to care what they say about me. I'm all alone and everyone thinks it's funny." Tears come to his eyes and he turns his face away from you. He is about to cry. What now?

(2) You've been tutoring Carlos, a fourth grade boy, at his school. He has made some academic progress in the last few weeks and the teacher says that it is because you have been giving him some extra help. You have enjoyed working with Carlos and it is obvious that he has become very fond of you.

You are his "special friend" and he looks forward to being with you because you not only help him with his studies, but you also talk with him about other matters. You even play with him on occasion. Last week you informed him that your meetings are about over and that you will not be coming to the school anymore.

This week, he tells you that he is not doing so well anymore and needs a lot more of your help. The teacher reports that since your last meeting, he has done no classwork and has become more disruptive. Carlos says to you: "Hey, why are you going to go away? I'm not doing so good anymore. My teacher says that I need more help. I want you to help me some more, okay?" What do you do now?

(3) You are meeting with Anna for the first time. She was reluctant to go with you to the conference room. You begin by asking a few simple questions in order to get the conversation going. However, Anna doesn't seem willing to share her ideas. After mumbling a few responses that were short and almost inaudible, she starts to stare out the window and look away at the walls. What is your next move?

(4) You and your co-leader have been meeting with a group of eighth grade students. Some of them look forward to being there, while a few seem to come only to get out of class. On this day, you both are trying a new activity. You are a little nervous and two students don't help matters when they begin to make side remarks and tell private jokes to each other. They are disruptive and you fear that you are going to lose control of the whole group unless you do something. What now?

(5) Your co-leader has planned an activity that you know will be fun to do with your ninth grade group. It is designed to help them think about their values. The activity goes well, but it only takes half the time that you planned. What might you do next?

(6) Your group is trying an activity that involves giving feedback. Felicia turns to Cindy and says: "I've been wanting to tell you this for a long time. You're conceited. All you think about is yourself and you never consider how the rest of us feel. We get tired of your being so 'uppity' and thinking that you are better than the rest of us. That's my feedback to you." Cindy doesn't say anything. The group is silent and it looks like they want you to do or say something. What will you do?

Activity 9.3:

ROLE PLAYING

PURPOSE:

To identify problem moments and role play possible responses.

MATERIALS:

Paper and pencil; any chairs or props that are appropriate for role playing situations.

PROCEDURE:

(1) The class is divided into three groups. Each group writes two problem moments, one for each of the other two groups.

(2) Each team then takes the two new problem moments and discusses among themselves how they will act out the problem. A "script" may be written which presents the key issues involved.

(3) Each team, in turn, role plays or acts out the problem moment. Allow about two to three minutes for each situation.

(4) Discussion follows regarding a) effectiveness and b) alternatives.

SELECTED REFERENCES

The following are selected references that have been cited or used in this book. A more complete listing of references and resources on the subject of peer faciltators and peer counselors can be found in the trainer manual, *Youth Helping Youth: A Handbook for the Training of Peer Facilitators*, that is a companion to this book.

Canfield, J. & Wells, H.C. *100 Ways to Enhance Self Concept in the Classroom.* Englewood Cliffs, NJ: Prentice-Hall, 1978.

Cross, G., Mryick R.D. & Wilkinson, G. "Communication Labs: A Developmental Approach," *School Counselor*, 1977, 24 (3), 186-191.

Daane, C. *Vocational Exploration Group (VEG).* Tempe, AZ: Studies for Urban Man,1972.

Bennett, G.K., Seashore, H.G. & Wesman, A.G. *The Differential Aptitude Test.* New York, NY: The Psychological Corporation, (5th Edition), 1974.

Dinkmeyer, D. *DUSO (Developing Understanding of Self and Others).* Circle Pines, MN: American Guidance Service,1970.

Gray, H.D. & Tindall, J. *Peer Power.* Muncie, IN: Accelerated Development, Inc.,1978.

Howe, L.W. & Howe, M.M. *Personalizing Education: Values Clarification and Beyond.* New York, NY: Hart Publishing Co., 1975.

Johnson, D. *Reaching Out.* Englewood Cliffs, NJ: Prentice-Hall, Inc.,1972.

Myrick, R.D., Erney, T. & Sorenson, D. *Peer Facilitators: Youth Helping Youth*, l6mm sound/color film. Minneapolis, MN: Educational Media Corporation,1976.

Orwell, G.*1984.* New York, NY: Signet,1971.

Palomares, U., Ball, G. & Bessell, H. *Magic Circle* (Human Development Program). La Mesa, CA: Human Development Training Institute,1970.

Pfeiffer, J.W. & Jones, J.E. *Structured Experiences for Human Relations Training.* La Jolla, CA: University Associates Press, 1972.

Purkey, W. *Self-concept and School Achievement.* Englewood Cliffs, NJ: Prentice-Hall,1970.

Rosenthal, R. & Jacobsen, L. *Pygmalion in the Classroom.* New York, NY: Holt, Rhinehart and Winston,1968.

Simon, S., Howe, L. & Kirschenbaum, H. *Values Clarification: A Handbook of Practical Strategies for Teachers and Students.* New York, NY: Hart Publishing Co.,1972.

Wittmer, J. & Myrick, R.D. *Facilitative Teaching: Theory and Practice.* Pacific Palisades, CA: Goodyear Publishing Co.,1974.